Two Go to Spain

Discovering Spain by Motorhome

John Laidler

Website: www.john-laidler.co.uk
Email: john@john-laidler.co.uk

"Among the biting wit you'll find plenty of travelling tips including details on off-the-beaten-track gems and the sights that really are worth battling with busloads of tourists to see."
Practical Motorhome Magazine

"There are plenty of travelogues from motorhomers heading out and about but few have the sheer number of maps and photos as Two Go to Spain....The couple and their dog are fairly inexperienced when they set off, which is where some of the entertainment comes from....an interesting read for anyone hoping to head for the continent in their motorhome or campervan."
MMM Magazine

Copyright

Contents

Introduction

This is a book about discovering Spain by motorhome. You don't need a motorhome to explore Spain of course, you can do that on a bicycle, a car or even on foot. This is a story about travel and places and the motorhome element is almost incidental.

We had been to Spain before. In earlier years tents and rented villas had provided shelter. Spain is not a stranger to me but it still has unexplored corners and the ability to surprise which is what this book is about. We started with the general idea of "going to Spain" but once we got there we began to realise there were parts, often encountered unexpectedly which were a delight to explore and there were other parts which for us were better skirted around. Except of course you have to go to these latter places first in order to realise what they are like. Writing this account of our travels is my way of sharing with you the variety and richness of Spain including, if only for completeness of course, a description of our visit to Benidorm, our encounters with mysterious masons' marks on stones, our discovery of some outstanding art and architecture and also, though this was not planned, our experience of the Spanish medical services when they are presented with broken bones.

The lessons we learned on our trips are not confined just to Spain. We have subsequently been up and down the length of Italy and we quickly realised we liked in Italy the very same type of places we liked in Spain. Unfortunately, we still kept stopping at places where we realised after a while we really shouldn't have bothered but this did at least give us an excuse to keep travelling and that is something everyone can enjoy for its own sake. Travelling is a joy but if you can go to nice places as well then it is even better. One day perhaps we will have reached a degree of expertise where we never visit anywhere regrettable. If we do you will probably never read about it as such a journey would make for very boring reading. Until that happens you will just have to read about our mistakes in books like this.

Some notes about the motorhome aspects of our trip have been included in an appendix at the back of the book. This section might go some way to satisfying the questions of current motorhomers and perhaps might help encourage a few others, the non-motorhoming muggles, to give this form of touring a try. There also a second appendix which lists all the places we stayed at just in case anyone really wants to follow in our steps.

The First Journey

Two Plus Dog into Spain

September and October, 2014

The Weather Decides our Route

This was our first overseas motorhome trip with our dog Bertie, a Jack Russell Terrier. Previously we had put him in kennels but as this trip was to be nearly six weeks long we decided he had to come with us, if only on financial grounds.

The trip was planned over the summer, during which time I researched places of interest and places to stay on a route which started at Santander on the north coast of Spain and then westward before dropping down through Portugal, exploring both the coast and the interior of the only major western European country I had not visited before. Unfortunately, the weather had other ideas and a few days before we were due to leave in the middle of September a massive depression firmly anchored itself off the west coast of Portugal, bringing rain and high winds to the region. The forecast suggested there was no prospect of it moving in the short term so we made a decision to head eastwards from Santander, dip into the Pyrenees and then drop down to the Mediterranean coast. This is why this account is called Two Plus Dog into Spain and not into Portugal.

It also demonstrates the great advantage of motorhoming. Like a snail you carry your home with you which means you can change direction, in our case a precise one hundred and eighty degree turn of direction and with little planning required other than turning to a new page of the road atlas.

There are two main options for getting to Spain in a vehicle. Driving through France from one of the Channel ports or taking one of the long ferries which depart from Portsmouth and Plymouth to Bilbao and Santander. There is endless debate in motorhoming circles on which is best. Financially, using one of the shorter crossings from Dover or Folkestone then driving down through France is generally the cheapest, unless you have a vehicle which uses a lot of fuel. Calais to the south of Spain can be done in about three full days of driving by the really determined but this option is singularly unattractive to us. An option for us would be to take the ferry across to Roscoff in Brittany from Plymouth, which we live on the outskirts of but this is not a cheap ferry and it would still leave us with a long drive down the west coast of France. This of course can be a delightful trip, I've cycled this coast from Spain to Brittany but you need to take at least a week over it. We have subsequently done this, but we had given ourselves on this trip just six weeks to explore Spain so we wanted to get there quickly, which is why we opted for the twenty hour voyage with Brittany Ferries from Plymouth to Santander. Quite why we only had six weeks for the trip is a different question and one which is a little hard to explain. The simple fact was we had had the motorhome only just over a year at this time and we were still learning, especially in terms of European travel. The previous September we had taken it to France and explored a bit of Brittany for a while before the arrival of cold weather persuaded us to go south to the Dordogne where we enjoyed very pleasant temperatures for a couple of weeks. We enjoyed the Dordogne although our first campsite there will always be remembered for the wrong reasons. When we woke up the first morning and looked out across the River Dordogne, beside which we were camped, we could see something green sticking up out of the water. It was the waders of an angler and regrettably he was still wearing them. The local fire brigade were called and they retrieved his body. Not a great introduction to motorhoming in France.

My wife Mary and I are both now retired and so in theory we could stay away much longer, there are motorhomers who spend every winter away but we chose a six week period as being sufficiently long to give us an opportunity to thoroughly explore some parts of Spain whilst being short enough to ensure there would be no danger of us growing bored. A weak excuse if you analyse it and subsequently our trips have grown longer, the most recent being eleven weeks which is just inside the ninety day limit when standard insurance policies start to get twitchy with your absence from the perceived safety of home shores.

For us the ferry from Plymouth to Santander is the most attractive way to get to Spain. It is a bit like flying there, you leave home; check in at the ferry port (a fifteen minute drive away from where we live) and after the boarding formalities and enjoying a pleasant time eating, drinking, sleeping and reading books on board you disembark the next day at your destination. But unlike an aircraft the ferry to Spain has the added and not insignificant bonus of offering the possibility of seeing whales and dolphins during the voyage.

We had originally intended to travel the first week in September but as I quickly found out this is also the time chosen by a lot of others and the ferry was full. We are not the only people it seems to have realised children go back to school at this time and prices everywhere are generally lower.

With only one sailing a week from Plymouth it was not until the Fourteenth of September when I could secure us a booking for ourselves, the motorhome and the dog.

On arrival at the port we handed over Bertie's passport together with our human ones and we were given a scanner to read the dog's microchip in return. When all was completed we were handed a yellow sticker with a picture of a dog kennel on it for the windscreen and then directed to our lane in the queue. It was soon clear this was going to be a busy ferry as there were lots of vehicles queuing and probably at least a hundred motorcycles as well.

I have boarded many ferries and the process is still something of a mysterious art, involving lines of disparate vehicles being called forward at random and the order in which you all arrived seems to have no relationship to the order in which you actually board. It makes sense of course to those directing operations but as a hapless and helpless participant it was a little disconcerting to find we were held back until almost the end. When we did finally board Brittany Ferries' flagship, the Pont Aven, the rear of our motorhome was only inches from the loading ramp after it had been raised

Once in the car deck there was someone to take us to the lift, the yellow sticker on the windscreen showed we were "with dog" and according to the rules all dogs are supposed to wear a muzzle outside of the kennels area but many dogs were not muzzled, especially those smaller dogs like ours which were being carried, though we did obey the rules being newcomers to all this. The lift took us as far up the ship as it could but we still had some stairs to climb to reach the kennels. Bertie had his own ticket; though he declined to carry it, but it showed his kennel number and the bar code on the ticket also opened the lock to get into the kennel area. We travelled on the same ship two years later and the crew then were much stricter about dogs being muzzled. Our experience with Bertie may not be typical of what you can expect now though muzzles are only required essentially for boarding and disembarkation, in between those times the dogs are not required to wear one when being exercised but they should be kept on a lead when out of their kennel. The kennels themselves were stainless steel and wholly devoid of any comfort, but we expected this and had brought bedding. There is a feeding dish attached to the inside of the kennel door with two compartments. We put water in one and left Bertie for an hour during which time we settled into our cabin before returning to give him a walk on deck and feed him. We fed Bertie on the deck with his own bowl then left him some dry biscuits in his kennel.

In the spirit of getting into the holiday mood as soon as possible we booked ourselves in for dinner at the Flora Restaurant, which is a cut above the cheaper and much more popular self-service restaurant. Unfortunately, as the ship was so full we could only get into the half past nine sitting but as they eat late in Spain in the evening we took this as an opportunity to get into practice.

A view of the kennels on the Pont Aven

We took Bertie for a couple of more walks on the deck before we went to sleep but he still refused to do anything with which dogs are normally associated with on walks. The following morning I rose early, prompted by the alarm on my mobile telephone, not realizing the too clever device had already set itself an hour ahead of ship time and so in darkness I took him for a prolonged walk with only a sailor for company who was hosing down the decks and the faintest smudge of sunlight on the horizon. Bertie was still resolved to break the world record for crossed legs, an impressive feat of bladder control for a man of his seventeen years. So after this further futile dog walk I went back to bed regretting the fact we hadn't brought tea making equipment with us. Later, Mary took him for a second walk at which point Bertie's resolve weakened and he finally cocked a leg, some twenty hours after the last occasion. Oceanographers may have noticed a small local rise in the sea level in the Bay of Biscay at this time.

The morning was further enlivened by a small pod of dolphins, probably Bottlenose Dolphins I think but I'm certainly no expert and records for the distribution of dolphin species in the Bay of Biscay should not be amended on my account. For the dog the morning was also enlivened by another event, but I will gloss over that on the grounds of delicacy. Suffice it to say the list to starboard was corrected with the use of a poo bag.

Dogs are allowed to be returned to your vehicle an hour before landing, which was fun, sharing a lift stuffed to the gunnels with slobbering dogs. Once he was safely back in the motorhome we returned upstairs and watched the ship enter Santander harbour in the sunshine.

Stepping into Spain

Santander is a naturally very sheltered port which looked at on a map reminds me of a stomach, if that is not too pointed an allusion for those who might arrive here after a rough crossing wishing they didn't have a stomach at all. There is a narrow entrance passage in the top right (looked at on the map) which opens up into a bag shaped main harbour which then narrows down towards the bottom before becoming thin and wriggly. The whole thing looks a bit like a human digestive tract which coincidentally also ends with a bottom.

The ferry stops alongside a wharf facing south east which is somewhat disorientating. Here you on the north coast of Spain and might expect to be able to look out over the sea towards an uninterrupted horizon but what you are faced with are mountains which just seem to be in the wrong place.

Mountains are something you quickly need to get used to in Spain. There are a lot of them though it has some vast flat plains as well where the rain is supposed to fall, though it doesn't confine itself to the plains as we were to find out. The rain in Spain is truly not discriminatory when it comes to deciding what sort of geological features it will visit with its moist bounty. You can get wet in Spain anywhere and this trip was to prove it was most likely to arrive shortly after we did.

As a natural harbour Santander has long been a port, it was known to the Romans and mentioned by Pliny the Elder and used as a commercial centre supporting mining activity further inland. It has had its fair share of dramatic events. In 1893 a ship unloading fifty tons of dynamite exploded killing over five hundred people and in 1941 a major fire destroyed virtually the entire medieval city centre and gutted the cathedral, an event which has left Santander with a decidedly modern feel, there being little of the old city left.

Though situated on a very rocky bit of coast Santander has some superb beaches and these have been hugely popular with the Spaniards from the Nineteenth Century onwards for the then new craze of sea bathing. The popularity of Santander improved further when Alfonso XIII built the impressive Palacio de la Magdalena in 1912. This building, which is now owned by the city of Santander and used as a meeting place and conference centre is positioned on the narrow headland jutting out into the entrance to the harbour and which can be seen to the north as the ferry enters the bay. Another interesting fact you might like to contemplate should you enter Santander on a ferry is on the opposite or south side of the channel from the Palacio is the little village of Pedreña. This is tucked away opposite the long sand spit and its claim to fame is that it was here that the golfer Severiano "Seve" Ballesteros was born in 1957.

Disembarkation seemed to take an age, last on also meaning last off this time though that is not always the case but once off we headed for Bilbao by the quickest route, which cost us about two Euros in tolls and was worth it for the quick and smooth run. The main road along the north coast of Spain is an impressive feat of engineering with numerous viaducts and tunnels and the section past Bilbao in particular seemed mainly underground at times as we passed through a succession of tunnels.

Our destination for the first night was a campsite at Mundaka, on the north coast between Bilbao and San Sebastian. The road here passes Guernica, the small town made famous by Picasso's depiction of the horrors inflicted on it by German dive bombers during the Civil War.

It was a good campsite in an excellent location by a sandy estuary but it had very small pitches and very, very steep hills and at twenty eight Euros a night it was to be the most expensive site we were to use on this trip which was not setting ourselves a very good example. But the facilities were clean and modern and the lady in reception spoke English which was something of a relief as my Spanish was *very* limited at this stage of the trip, not that it was to improve much. Our arrival at the site didn't go smoothly as the book we were using had both the coordinates of the camp and the description how to find it incorrect, but find it we did in the end.

(As an aside, the details of where we stayed each night are all listed in Appendix 2 at the back of the book.)

After our first night in Spain, which was uneventful after the minor drama of actually finding the site, we set off for the Pyrenees the following morning. This of course was still in completely the opposite direction to the one we had intended to take when planning the trip at home but the storms were still hitting the far west of the Iberian Peninsula so our best course of action was to continue running away from them.

I like the Pyrenees having fallen in love with them many years ago as a child when we toured as a family towing a camping trailer made by my father. A place we returned to more than once was the Ordesa National Park which is roughly in the middle of the Pyrenees on the Spanish side. This has some of the most striking mountain scenery I have ever seen. A sort of European Grand Canyon. The Saiq Plateau in

Oman, for example, has some beetling cliffs which I've stood on but I think Ordesa has them beaten.

We passed Pamplona and then along narrow roads we climbing up into the foothills of the Pyrenees, finally arriving close to the end of the tarmac road at the head of the Anso Valley, where our intention was to spend a few days walking and bird watching. We were certainly now well off the popular tourist track. The site here, beside the Rio Veral and in an area of the Pyrenees known as the Western Valleys, is not listed in many books and I only knew about it because I had seen it earlier in the same year when my brother and I over fourteen days cycled the length of the Pyrenees, from Girona to San Sebastian.

Camping Zuriza in the Anso Valley

It struck me then as a place I needed to return to. And here we were. The next day we walked eastward up a side valley of the Rio Veral, the Barranco de Petrafiche. There was some impressive geology above us. We followed a gravel track which ran at first beside the river before crossing it at a bridge after which it began climb slowly up through the trees. Eventually it levelled out where there were some fields and here we found griffon vultures circling around and coming into land just the other side of a ridge near us. We rushed forward and I was rewarded with the best view of these vultures I had seen.

Typical Pyrenean scenery - the Barranco de Petrafiche

There must have been at least thirty of them but whatever had attracted them here didn't last very long because no sooner had they gathered than they quickly began to disperse, though not before I managed to get a photograph of one group standing around looking as miserable as only vultures can when they are contemplating whatever meal it was they had missed.

A little while later Mary nearly stood on an adder which was lying on the track. Don't believe stories that say adders will get out of your way, they don't all and this one just lay there. It was almost certainly feeling very cold and was warming itself in the weak sun. Given it had clearly no intention of trying to move we had to carefully walk around it. To confirm the chilled reptile theory we subsequently came across a large toad doing exactly the same a little further on. It completely ignored us and just lay there with its stomach pressed to the ground.

There was no danger of our dog Bertie standing on anything which might bite back because Bertie wasn't with us. Bertie was seventeen years old and a long walk for him was twice around the motorhome. So if you don't read much about Bertie in the following pages it is because he slept through most of it.

Unfortunately, our attempts to outrun the bad weather soon started to unravel when cold air arrived and low cloud set in all around us. So we decided to abandon our plan to explore the Pyrenees and headed south instead for some sun. This wasn't a decision we took lightly as I had really wanted to move after our current location to the Ordesa National Park further to the east, but striking mountain scenery is not much use if you can't see it due to low cloud.

Griffon vultures, not the prettiest but magnificent in flight

The route we took in our retreat from the mountains used some fairly minor roads and slowly we came to realize there was a lot more to Spain than the highlights in the guide book. This was to become a theme of much of both this trip and the one we were to take the following year. If you take more or less any minor road in Spain sooner or later you will pass through somewhere interesting. The real trick, and we still haven't completely mastered it, is having found somewhere interesting to actually stop and enjoy the place.

As an example, on our way south from the Pyrenees we suddenly and unexpectedly came across some spectacular red cliffs between Puente la Reina de Jaca and Huesca.

These are known as *Los Mallos* (the mallets) *de Riglos* and their intricate and vertical faces attract skilled climbers.

The *Los Mallos de Riglos*

From a distance it looks like sandstone but it is a conglomerate or mixture of rocks with boulders embedded in it varying in size between "a tennis ball and a microwave" according to the description on a climbing website I looked at. It was a remarkable discovery for us but we didn't stop as we had already decided our destination for the day and so we kept going. The lesson on being flexible enough to stop, there is a village with parking beside the rocks we could have stayed the night, had not yet been learned. How long would it take us to realise this?

The Mediterranean

Our journey to the sea was done in one day and covered some three hundred and fifty kilometres. Not exactly the relaxing sort of driving I prefer but we had been decidedly cold during our last night in the mountains and the attractions of the promised warmth on the coast were a strong spur to going as far south as reasonably possible in a day.

Our destination was a campsite a little north of Valencia near the town of Sagunto where for an extra couple of Euros we could have a pitch just behind the beach.

The weather was warm but with a nice breeze off the sea to keep us cool. This was also the first warm weather Bertie had experienced on the trip and we were not sure how he would cope. We need not have worried; he spent most of each day lying on the floor of the motorhome in front of the twelve volt fan, only waking as the cool of evening arrived. He liked the fan so much we had to place shoes against it to stop him leaning up against it and blocking the airflow.

Bertie asleep in front of the *Endless Breeze* fan

But yet again the weather changed after a few days of lazing by the beach, the sun ran away and was replaced by heavy rain so we drove further south down the coast to Alicante, with a minor detour near Benidorm when we turned inland to visit Guadalest and its famous castle where we found ourselves surrounded by bus loads of tourists.

We decided to stay at a campsite north of Alicante, just behind Campello Beach for a couple of nights. This was in a very urban setting, which felt more than a little strange. My previous experience of campsites had led me to think they were all surrounded by countryside. This one was surrounded by high rise buildings. Of course when originally built it may well have been in the countryside but the relentless rise of tourism and the growth in accommodation and facilities for tourists has left it marooned in a sea of modern buildings.

The site also had a feature new to me, lonely British men. They probably wouldn't consider themselves lonely but that is how they appeared to us. The principal identification feature of these gentlemen is once engaged in conversation it is very hard to escape from them. There was one particular man who took a shine to us but fortunately he was in the process of moving to another site nearby so the preparation for the move took up much of his time as he had so much stuff to move. He had a caravan and a large van in a corner of the site which he had effectively made his own. The van was nothing more than a giant wardrobe, we glimpsed inside it one day and the whole of the cargo area was full of clothing; suits, trousers and shirts by the dozen. No doubt there were boxes of shoes in there as well. The biggest problem for his move, all of about five hundred metres, was the logistics because his van was uninsured and had neither been taxed or had anything resembling an MOT or road-worthiness certificate. These had long since expired as he had been in Spain several years but he felt if he moved during the early hours of the morning he would be safe. He would also probably have to make at least two journeys as he had collected so much around him in his little corner of England, including white plastic fencing, wooden outside flooring and a large swing with a two person seat suspended from it. I wonder if the campsite he was moving to knew just what they were letting themselves in for? But he was a pleasant chap and I hope his move went off smoothly.

While at this site we noticed for the first time Bertie wasn't quite fully aware of what was going on around him. The incident which stood out was when he wandered over to a parked car and barked at the driver's door to be let in. It wasn't our car but obviously he thought it was.

As might be expected we were not left in sunshine for long and before long some truly Biblical weather caught up with us. Thunder and lightning during the night and in the morning a huge funnel cloud ("waterspout") stretching from the sea to the clouds appeared just off the coast. It only lasted about a minute and I wasn't able to get a decent photograph of it but after these ill omens we decided to move yet further south. It didn't help when one of the long term residents of the site told us this was the first rain he had seen in nine months. We felt it prudent not to tell him it had rained wherever we had stopped so far on this holiday and perhaps it wouldn't have here either if we had not arrived dragging our own private storm with us.

So where to go for the best chance of sun and warmth? The most arid part of Spain is inland from Almeria, where the *Desierto de Tabernas* can be found with an annual rainfall so low it is classed as a desert, Europe's only true desert. It was here Sergio Leone made his three famous *Man with no name* westerns starring Clint Eastwood and the sets which were created for the films are now theme parks, which is a very good reason to stay away from them but we could at least approach the area and try and experience some of the legendary dryness.

We chose a campsite close to the coastal town of Águilas, which is famous for a wild fiesta in February and is relatively undeveloped compared to many other places on this coast either side of it.

As might be expected, despite the famed aridity of the region after a day or so of fine weather the thunderstorms caught up with us yet again and on our last night we had the most intense display of lightening which went on for several hours. It was a good job Bertie was more or less deaf but there was no doubt it was time to move on despite the entertainment value of the thunderstorms.

Our route south west hugged the coast for part of the way and a little way past Garrucha we stopped for lunch at a place where you could drive right onto the beach. An extraordinary motorhome was already parked here, Swiss registered and based on a military eight wheel drive truck. It had a roof which could be raised to expose the windows. I think it was a bit of overkill as we had no problem getting onto the beach but if you wanted to drive overland in Africa or Asia I guess it would be excellent.

Our 'van with the military motorhome with rising roof behind

How they manage to park it in Lidl's for shopping will remain a mystery. I have subsequently heard it belongs to a Swiss gentleman who runs a company making complimentary medicine and he comes to Spain each winter to dream up new products. It must be a profitable business as I doubt his vehicle cost anything less than a million Euros and possible two or more millions. We eventually stopped a little east of Motril and more or less directly south from Granada. This turned out to be a fairly unattractive stretch of coast with vast areas turned over to intensive horticulture in plastic tunnels. Our campsite itself was hemmed in by these plastic greenhouses on both sides and with a rather narrow shingle beach on the south side and a characterless village to the north it wasn't a site which was immediately attractive although the welcome was warm enough. With a strong wind blowing and intermittent rain it felt like being in the Lake District when we sat down in the evening to our first supper of bacon and eggs on the trip so far.

The weather forecast was more of the same damp weather for the next day or so but then dry for most of the following week before the rains returned. This was not the southern Spain I was expecting. But on the positive side I was still wearing shorts.

What we were experiencing is what the Spanish call a *Gota fria* or "cold drop" which is not uncommon along the Spanish Mediterranean coast in the autumn and occurs when the sea is warm but the upper atmosphere becomes cold. The characteristic thunder and lightning generated is often accompanied by localized flooding. September up until the middle of October is prime times for these events, coinciding perfectly with our holiday.

We stayed only one night near Motril, a decidedly unattractive area and kept going west with the intention of going about as far south as we could.

Our Rough Guide to Spain guidebook paints a rude picture of the Costa del Sol, which is what we travelled though, but the bits we saw from the motorway looked quite upmarket, including some swish developments around golf courses. I suspect the coastal strip is a bit different but we didn't fancy the inevitable stop/start drive along the coastal road so we swept past Marbella and Algeciras, glimpsing Gibraltar through the humidity and turned right at Tarifa, there being no real alternative at this southernmost tip of Spain unless you want to cross over to Morocco.

The Atlantic Coast

From Tarifa we went just 10km north along the coast to a campsite near Valdevaqueros behind a huge sandy beach which seemed to be the kite surfing capital of Europe. There were literally well over a hundred of them being used and the air was filled with their sails scooting at speed in all directions.

The coast running north from Tarifa is the Costa de la Luz or coast of light, so named because of the brightness of the beaches under the sunlight. It even looked as if it was going to live up to its name because the weather finally seemed to have decided to remain sunny although a disturbing number of clouds built up on our first evening.

We found an excellent pitch at Camping Valdevaqueros which was mainly grass and shaded by trees which would be welcome if we got better weather, we could but hope. Things improved further when a party of fifty school children camped in the tent area on the other side

23

from us packed up and left just after we arrived. Hopefully, their departure was pre-planned and not due to our arrival. It was after all Sunday evening and this seems more believable than they had received advanced notice of our rain-bearing gifts.

We spent three nights at Valdevaqueros but it wasn't all lazing in the sunshine we did take a taxi into Tarifa for half a day's sightseeing where we treated ourselves to lunch. They are big on tuna here, which are caught in the Straits of Gibraltar so we couldn't pass on a bit of grilled tuna and very nice it was too. Tarifa is worth a walk around; it has a central old quarter behind the original city walls which isn't too touristy.

Tarifa viewed from the Isla de las Palomas

We also discovered Tarifa was indeed the kite surfing capital of Europe with numerous shops selling and renting equipment. What draws the surfers here isn't just the beaches but the wind. Tarifa has another claim to fame, it has historically had a very high suicide rate and the relentless winds which blow at times are considered to be a factor in this unenviable statistic. Not unlike the stories of the *mistral* in France driving people to take their own lives. It is also a very good area for wind turbines and these covered many of the coastal hillsides.

24

Near where we had lunch there was a large statue to *Guzman el Bueno* (Guzman the Good) who was a hero of the siege of Tarifa in 1294. The statue shows a grim mail-clad figure clutching a large dagger. The legend says Guzman's nine year old son was captured and threatened with death if Guzman did not surrender the city. Guzman's choice was "honour without son over dishonour with son" and he threw down his dagger so the attackers could use it to kill his own son. Tarifa had been an early conquest of the Moors but it had been liberated by this time and the siege, though it used Moorish forces, was led by a rebellious faction of Sancho the son of the then king Alfonso X. Guzman's example was to be followed many centuries later when during the Spanish Civil War the commander of the garrison of Toledo was threatened with the death of his own son if he did not surrender. He took the Guzman choice though his son was not killed immediately but about a month later in reprisals for an air raid by Franco's forces.

When we left, heading north west, we explored a bit of the coast, driving through the national park north west of Barbate. This was full of Stone or Umbrella Pines (*Pinus pinea*) which are distributed all around the Mediterranean and have been cultivated since prehistoric times for their edible seeds.

Umbrella pines

These days some twenty species of pine are used to produce "pine nuts" or seeds for sprinkling on salads but *Pinus pinea* was the original source. The trees have a distinctive domed top. Unfortunately, I nearly got bogged in when I stopped to take the photograph above. Memo to self: do not drive onto sand no matter how firm it looks. Fortunately, we escaped after a few nervous moments of wheel spinning but we now carry some fibreglass sand ladders to put under the wheels should we ever find ourselves in such a position again. Of course having bought the sand ladders it probably means we will never need them, but at least we are prepared if we do.

Lunch was at the end of the road past the Playa de Zahora, which is a naturist beach. It was blowing very hard off the land and the thermometer touched thirty degrees. I dread to think what bits were being sandblasted on the beach, which was probably why most of the naturists seemed to be packing up and going home.

Since we had left Águilas we had been travelling through Andalusia, the most south westerly region of Spain. The name derives from the Arabic *Al-Andalus* first recorded on coins dating from around 715 but scholars disagree on what it actually means. However, it is a very varied region but one very characteristic feature of Andalusia are the white villages, the *Pueblos Blancos* and one of the more well-known is Vejer de la Frontera. Like the other white villages this is perched for defensive purposes on a hill which is reached by a steep and twisty road. Fortunately in this case they are used to tourists here so there is a large car park near the top of the road where we could leave the motorhome and explore the narrow streets of the old town on foot. In the picture below, which shows the new part of the town from the ramparts of the old you can see the white houses but also a curious statue. This is the *Cobijada*, Vejeca's famous "covered lady". The figure depicts a style of dress made up of two parts, the upper *manto* which covers the head and upper part of the body and the lower *saya* which was a loosely gathered skirt around the waist. *Cobijada* clothing was banned during the Spanish Civil War as it could be used to conceal the carriage of weapons but it was still being worn by a few ladies until the second half of the Twentieth Century. More recently the costume has seen a revival and there is an annual competition held in Vejar to crown a junior and senior *Cobijada* of the year.

This was an interesting visit and a cold beer afterwards on a shady terrace in the old part of the town made the day.

Our stop for the night was a campsite at El Puerto de Santa María, across the bay from Cadiz. It was a large and well organised site but somewhat lacking in shade and it had biting insects. We should have taken the hint when we found ourselves the only people sitting out as it got dark.

Vejer de la Frontera and the *Cobijada* Lady

Mary was badly bitten and itched for days afterwards. This was a painfully learned lesson and one which we have tried hard not to forget on subsequent trips. If other people are sitting out in the evening then it is probably safe to do the same yourself. If you see everyone scuttling inside and closing windows, beware. Mosquitoes are not such a problem in they haven't developed the stealth attack some other biting insects have. The problem here at El Puerto de Santa María was whatever was doing the biting was silent, very small and the bites were initially painless so you simply had no way of telling you were under attack until you surveyed the wounds on your ankles the following morning. The insects doing the biting were probably some sort of sand fly, of which there are several species, most belonging to the sub-family *Phlebotominae* a name which is a bit of a give-away as to their habits when you remember the nurse who collects blood samples is known as a Phlebotomist. But losing blood to these insects is the least thing to worry about, like mosquitoes they can carry harmful diseases and in the case of sand flies the main worry is Leishmaniasis which is potentially fatal. In the daytime you don't generally need to worry about them as the insects are principally nocturnal and start emerging at dusk. Which is just the time we like sitting out. Our standard technique now if we think there just might be biting creatures is to wear socks if at all possible (yes, I know, with sandals, a terrible fashion crime but our excuse is it is dark so no one can see) and burn mosquito coils just upwind of our feet. We also use some sort of repellent and have found the Scottish midge-buster *Smidge* excellent providing you slap plenty of it on. This regime generally seems to work but it is still possible to get caught out. Of course it would be much safer to go inside every evening but to us this would mean missing one of the true pleasures of travelling, being able to sit out in the warmth of an evening, reading or talking and enjoying a glass of wine.

The next morning we took the ferry to Cadiz and did the touristy thing. The map we had obtained from the campsite reception office showed suggested routes delineated on the page by different coloured lines. Initially I found it a little difficult to follow these as the detail and scale on the map was a little variable. Then we noticed the same coloured lines had been drawn on the street, which made things just a little easier to follow. In the photograph on the next page you may be able see one of these lines running along the side of the street.

A street in Cadiz showing the coloured lines you follow to tour the city

Cadiz is very touristy and there was a big cruise liner docked, the *Thomson Dream* which must have disgorged several hundred if not the odd thousand onto the streets. It was still worth seeing Cadiz but it is not the sort of place we would want to go back to immediately.

The day after our trip to Cadiz we walked into Puerto de Santa Maria from the campsite for a bit of sightseeing. Compared to Cadiz this is a small town but it is a working town with some very distinctive architecture in the some of the streets around the sherry bodegas. It has a pleasant castle with the remains of a stork's nest on it, a bull ring with freshly raked sand in the ring though no sign of bulls, alive or otherwise, and a few weather-beaten churches. Like Cadiz the older buildings have been made from a soft rock which weathers in the salt laden air of the coast.

A busy street scene in Cadiz

Santa Maria is the southern corner of the sherry triangle, the other corners being Sanlúcar de Barrameda in the north, where *manzanilla* sherry comes from and inland and forming the eastern corner, Jerez de la Frontera, where the bulk of sherry is produced. The name Jerez is itself the origin of the word sherry. The location of the two coastal towns is supposed to imbue their sherries with a taste of salt. I must admit, having had a few bottles of *manzanilla* in my time I have never detected any salt but if were ever to taste salty sherry we were in no better place to try – so we arranged a visit to a sherry bodega. The name bodega is derived from the term for a wine cellar, initially from the Greek (*apotheke*) then through Latin (*apoteca*) and thus to Spanish, possibly, and this is only my own pet theory, through Arabic because there is no letter "p" in standard Arabic, where it is usually replaced by the letter "b".

We had very nice tour, in English, with a good explanation of the sherry making process followed by a leisurely tasting of five different sherries poured in generous portions, all for six Euros. Refreshingly, there was absolutely no hard sell to buy anything, though of course we did because we both like sherry, *fino* for me but the other half was converted to *oloroso*, which was fine, we just needed to find room in the refrigerator for the his and hers bottles. We did learn a new trick during the sherry tasting and it involved salt which we still couldn't taste in the sherry but we could taste it in the peanuts and crisps they served with the drinks. The extra salt helps appreciate the wine we were told and being partial to both peanuts and crisps we were not going to argue.

Sherry is a blend of wines from several different years. Both port and sherry are fortified wines in that additional alcohol is added after the initial fermentation and the resulting mix is then put in a barrel. With port that is normally more or less the end of the process apart from a later stage of bottling; this depending on the style of port can be after a long or short time in the barrel. Counter-intuitively, and unlike say whiskey, the most expensive ports spend the least amount of time in the barrel, being allowed to mature in the bottle which being sealed from the air takes much longer than ports which are left in the barrel. However, some port and a number of other wines including Madeira and Muscat are also produced using the same process as is used for all sherry, the *solera* process which a system of fractional blending. *Solera* means "on the ground" in Spanish and refers to the lowest barrel holding the oldest sherry and which is the one used for bottling. In the picture below you can see three rows of barrels. Sherry is drawn off from the bottom row and replenished by sherry drawn from the row above which in turn is topped up by sherry from the upper row. The sherry from the top row is then replaced with the product of the new harvest.

Sherry *solera*

With just three rows of barrels you might think the best you could get from this system is sherry aged three years, but this would be wrong. A *solera* of three rows where half a barrel is drawn off from the bottom barrel each year will produce sherry averaging nearly five years old. For the mathematicians the average age of the sherry approaches asymptotically the figure given by the formula:

$$1 + ((R - 1)/f)$$

Where "R" is the number of rows and "f" is the fraction of a barrel drawn off each year. So in the example given above the figure 5 is arrived at by $1 + ((3-1)/0.5) = 1 + (2/0.5) = 1 + 4 = 5$

Unusually, sherry barrels are left open to the atmosphere, allowing a degree of oxidation which adds to the distinctive flavour. A further complication in the process is some sherries spontaneously develop a different character and turn from a *fino* sherry to an *oloroso*, with a darker appearance and different taste. This is a consequence of the barrels being open to the air.

The bodega we visited, *Gutierrez-Colosia*, is one of the smaller sherry producers but the premium wines they sell are sold in some very upmarket restaurants including Noma in Copenhagen which has been voted the best restaurant in the world on several occasions. Unfortunately, it seems the supply of these special sherries will end eventually as the company was bought a few years ago and it was the new owners who found several large barrels of aged sherry gathering dust and cobwebs. These were tasted and promptly put on the market at a substantial price. We were also shown a special row of barrels where the contents had already been sold and the names of the purchasers were written on the front of the barrels in chalk. There were several well-known chefs listed amongst them. We felt somewhat privileged and a bit cheapskate as we slunk out with three bottles from the cheaper end of their range. But we needn't have worried, the Spanish are really not snobbish about sherry and the proper way to buy your everyday drinking sherry is to turn up at the *bodega* with a plastic bottle and ask them to fill it. There were at least two people who came in to do this as we were selecting our meagre few bottles.

When we came out of the bodega after the sherry tasting it was late morning, the sun was shining strongly and we tried our very best to walk back to the campsite in a straight line without giggling. If you are ever in the region don't miss out on a sherry tasting tour of a *bodega* and if possible go on several but probably not on the same day and ideally later in the day would be better and even then schedule in a long *siesta* afterwards.

You can visit bodegas all over the sherry triangle, some of the most well-known *Gonzalez Byass* and *Pedro Domecq* are in Jerez de la Frontera but if you want to escape the crowds and try something a little different and taste sherries you won't find in your local supermarket it is worth seeking out the smaller producers.

Seville

Seville is most certainly not off the beaten track but we had heard and read so much about it having now arrived in the bottom right hand corner of Spain we decided to visit. In fact you can't really avoid Seville if like us you are travelling up the coast towards Portugal because the north side of the sherry triangle is delineated by the Guadalquivir river and the marshlands of the Coto Doñana where it flows into the sea, through which there are no publicly accessible roads so you are inevitably pushed up towards Seville.

It is possible to find aires in Seville but we chose a campsite on the edge of the city, one of the oldest in Spain and still owned by the original family. The age of the site probably explains why the pitches were tiny, it had been designed for tents but we squeezed into a space and settled in. Opposite us was something we hadn't so far noticed, someone living in a small tent. Subsequently, perhaps because we knew what to look for, we saw this more often and realised it was a sign of the state of the Spanish economy. We hardly saw the owner of the tent, they left on a bicycle early in the morning, arrived back late and then after cooking a meal went to sleep. Wherever the man's family was I suspected it was a long way from Seville but at least he seemed to have found work here, which is more than many in Spain have where youth unemployment is around forty percent, beaten only by the unenviable figure from Greece where it is fifty percent.

The helpful guy in reception, who spoke near perfect English, gave us directions to the bus stop so the day after arriving we took a local bus into Seville. If we were not already prepared for the crowds by the number of tourists waiting at the bus stop with us we were sharply reminded of Seville's popularity as soon as we arrived. The bus stopped in what can only be called "tourist bus stop street number one". There were numerous tourist buses disgorging their passengers at the same place and the same people then immediately all more or less headed in the same direction towards the main sites of the old city on the east bank of the Guadalquivir.

Seville has, if you are doing the rapid shore run from your cruise ship, three main "don't miss" sights: the Giralda Tower, the cathedral (*Catedral*) and the Alcázar.

The queue for the Alcázar, the traditional seat of the rulers of Seville was at least two hundred yards long and not perceptibly moving. With a hot sun beating down we decided that the lure of the Alcázar and the other two main attractions could wait.

We did find one place where there were no queues, the Hospicio de los Venerables, a former rest home for elderly priests which was opened towards the end of the Eighteenth Century. Though no doubt lacking the wow factor of other buildings in Seville it had some wonderful features and is strongly recommended. In the centre was a delightful courtyard or patio where water was collected for use in the hospice. The main part of the building, set around a cool courtyard which also collected rainwater now houses works of art from the 17th century including a couple of lesser works by Velázquez.

Courtyard of the Hospicio de los Venerables

In one corner was a wonderful little church with a 20th century organ used for recitals of work by Bach etc., which would be very atmospheric to hear I think given the location. The church itself had some elaborate decoration on the walls and ceiling - not a drop of magnolia to be seen though there were a few cracks which needed filling.

There was an entrance fee of about five Euros but for that you were given an audio guide which contained more information than we could handle, especially about the paintings but the guide did help to make sense of what we were seeing.

Ceiling of the church at the Hospicio de los Venerables

This fresco (next page) by Juan de Valdés Leal is painted on a flat ceiling. The sense of perspective he achieved is superb.

Afterwards we had a leisurely lunch at a roadside table in a busy street near the Hospicio. It cost a little under twelve Euros for four decent sized tapas and a couple of glasses of wine each at a price which seemed good value for Seville.

After a bit more wandering and a stop for a sorbet we caught the bus back to the campsite, which we almost overshot. The bus plays a nice trick; it doesn't stop anywhere near where you got on and approaches the campsite from a completely different direction. Just look for; palm trees growing in sand beside the road is all I can suggest if you follow our faltering steps.

Walking around cities is hard work so the next day we moved again for some rest, this time to Isla Cristina just short of the Portuguese border. Here we found a somewhat unexciting campsite with more than its share of flies but it did have a very good beach, clean sand and shallow water which we more or less had to ourselves. There was also a troupe of Azure Winged Magpies in the site which flew around looking for mischief. In the evening we heard some very interesting bird song in the trees above us but the birds at first refused to come out into the open and be identified but eventually one did and they were Spotless Starlings, which is the variety you get here in Spain. Not uncommon by any means but wonderful singers with a very varied repertoire.

Extraordinary _trompe l'oeil_ effect

We arrived at Isla Cristina via the Coto Doñana, the huge national park at the mouth of the Guadalquivir where we made a diversion to the town of El Rocio which was packed, there must have been three hundred cars parked around the church and numerous buses as well. El Rocio is effectively a pilgrimage town composed of buildings for 'Hermandades' from almost every town in Spain. The word _Hermandades_ comes from the Spanish for "brotherhood" and these organisations are descended from local militia who in medieval times kept the peace. Some of the first to be formed were along the pilgrimage route to Santiago de Compostela to protect the pilgrims, who were an important source of income for the villages through which the pilgrims passed.

The _Hermandades_, sometimes two or three different ones each day are allowed to parade their icons around the town ending up at the very large church. Being in Spain this is accompanied by lots of noise and huge rockets like coastguard maroons let off by hand. Bands composed of people and often many children bang drums with one hand while playing a tin whistle with the other. Pentecost is the major festival when up to half a million people make the pilgrimage from all over Spain and camp around the town. A festival which is not without its criticism due partly to the environmental impact of so many vehicles and people in a sensitive area and also because of reports of cruelty to animals with a reported twenty three horses dying in 2009.

El Rocio - note the huge church

To Portugal and Back

Having travelled to the Portuguese border it would have been a waste not to visit, especially as this was a country neither of us had been to before.

The Algarve is famously popular amongst the British and this was very obvious when we stopped to do some shopping. There were English voices almost everywhere and the shop assistants spoke a bit too. Which was very helpful as my knowledge of Portuguese was and remains zero. Written down it looks quite a bit like Spanish but this is misleading as the spoken word is totally different. On first hearing Portuguese spoken we both thought we had suddenly been transported to Eastern Europe, so alien did it sound.

Of course we first had to get into Portugal and being in a hurry as usual we decided to use the motorway, which is a toll road. For a country which perhaps unfairly has a reputation for being somewhat undeveloped Portugal has one of the most modern toll systems in Europe with automatic number plate recognition cameras mounted on gantries above the motorway. For this to work the system needs to know who the car belongs to and have a means of automatically charging the vehicle owner.

As we crossed into Portugal a sign directed us to a lane marked "Foreign Vehicles" which ended at an automatic barrier with a large machine beside it. There was no sign of anyone around but I expected this so I jumped out and attempted to offer the machine my bank card. It wasn't playing, indeed the machine looked so completely blank it was as if the electricity had been cut off. Was Portugal's economy in that bad a state?

The solution came from Mary when she suggested perhaps we were not close enough to the barrier. So I edged a little closer and suddenly the machine lit up as though we had won the jackpot in Las Vegas. The problem was the vehicle had not been close enough to the camera to allow it to both recognize it had a customer (and wake up) and be able to read our number plate.

After this we had the freedom to roam Portugal's' extensive motorway network, which was a pleasant experience as we more or less had it to ourselves. The problem, which is well known though no one in Portugal seems to want to do anything about it, is the Portuguese road tolls are so high no local, or almost no local uses them, so all Portuguese vehicles confine themselves to the old roads leaving the motorways free to be used by visitors in a hurry.

Of course there was no particular reason to be in a hurry as we had plenty of time but the idea of creeping along the coast road from resort to resort did not appeal though we probably missed out on some interesting places by our dash to the west. The weather was overcast so with no incentive to stop early to do some sunbathing we just kept driving and eventually we ended up at Figueira in the western Algarve, about ten kilometres short of the south western tip of Portugal. Or to put it another way we drove west along the bottom of Portugal until we could more or less go no further.

We stayed at a small privately owned camping park, which had only just been completed and had been open only a few months. Unfortunately, we were the only ones there, which was a bit sad for the owners who had clearly invested quite a bit of money in the venture. By Portuguese standards it was not the cheapest aire at seven and a half Euros a night but it was very conveniently positioned on the edge of the village and near an excellent beach. Don't be fooled by the old VW parked in the shot below. It was empty and was a decoy to lure in the passing trade.

The only thing to take the shine off the place (apart from the weather, more of which later) was it had something of a dog problem, of the loud barking variety right next door type of dog problem.

The camper park at Figueira

Fortunately, the noisy animals remained silent most of the time only waking up to bark when a stranger appeared, which wasn't *too* often. There was also a cockerel keeping the dogs company but it wasn't very loud either so if you are fan of Old MacDonald or just like animals these distractions are not really a problem and must be an aid to security.

Unfortunately, the bad weather had not been fooled by our change of country and it soon caught up with us as we woke to heavy rain the following morning and were subsequently caught in a couple of showers in the afternoon when we went for a walk. Regrettably, the long distance forecast didn't look very clever for the next four days or so either. We weren't going to see much sun in these parts until the following week, our last full week in Spain and during which we needed to start heading back.

A further night of heavy rain followed and the forecast was of more rain during the day. Things were not looking good weather-wise. Which was a shame; we had hardly done more than catch a glimpse of Portugal and the touristy Algarve at that. There was a whole new country further north and if we are ever to get away from the crowds in Europe there are few better places to try than Portugal, with the exception of the Algarve of course and the major cities. You can see the dark skies in the photograph above and this one of the village of Figueira. The camper park we were staying in is in the bottom left near the little blue building.

Figueira under threatening skies

Return to Spain

The problem with the aire at Figueira was not the animal noises which we could live with but that it was built on a red earth. They had put white chippings down on the pitches but it was a very thin coating and the ground was soft in places. When we walked the dog he needed his feet washing in a bowl before he could get back into the motorhome if we didn't want the interior of the 'van looking like a painting from Picasso's terracotta period. With more rain forecast for the weekend, up to an inch on Saturday apparently, we admitted defeat and scuttled back to Seville to stay at an aire next to the river and hopefully high enough above it to be safe should the rain forecast for Portugal overshoot and land here. We had come to the marina at Gelves on the south western outskirts of Seville where the marina owners had set aside a paved strip along the river bank for motorhome parking. We had a book listing aires in Spain and it said there was an attractive looking restaurant within the marina. Which I can't disagree with in regards looks except it didn't sell attractive looking food, just a very slim range of warm tapas which no one seemed to be eating sitting in trays on the bar, like a buffet. We also couldn't find a restaurant in the immediate neighbourhood so with plans to eat out scuppered Mary knocked up a chorizo and chickpea stew which was very nice although the Portuguese sourced chorizo were singularly lacking in any chilli heat.

Having "done" Seville already on this trip we decided to stay only the single night and move on the next day to Ronda, which had always been on the list of places to visit on this trip. Of course, just to keep us on our toes we had the inevitable thunder and lightning show during our night halt. This made the place feel almost like home.

I later discovered October is statistically the wettest month in many parts of Spain, November and December being drier though a lot cooler. Warm and wet or cool and dry. Take your pick but we prefer dry *and* warm whenever possible.

But I digress, back at the aire at Gelves there were no obvious drains for waste water and the only alternative was the toilet emptying point, a sinister oubliette under a metal cover some distance away in the boat park. Somehow I don't think many people used this for emptying waste water as the lush vegetation around the water points was a good indication the majority used the expedient of just chucking their waste onto the grass. On the plus side the water and electric points were numerous and the 'van was on hard standing and there didn't seem to be a biting insect problem. Possibly that was due to the weather but the river here was tidal and moved at a fair pace at times so I doubt it is a popular breeding ground for insects. Alternatively, this being a city perhaps there were so many targets for any insects to choose from we were left alone?

After breakfast we headed south, avoiding the toll road by taking an alternative toll-free route. As it seemed did everyone else. It wasn't hard to spot the junction, just follow the line of trucks as they peeled off. It isn't just in Portugal drivers avoid the toll roads where they can though the absence of traffic on the Portuguese motorways was striking.

The rain set in with some determination not long after we started and it continued, at times very heavily until lunch, which was convenient. I prefer it to rain at night but if rains during the day it is nice when it stops for meal times.

Our route to Ronda was not the direct one our satnav wanted us to take, which had her loudly complaining until I turned off the sound, leaving her to fume in silence.

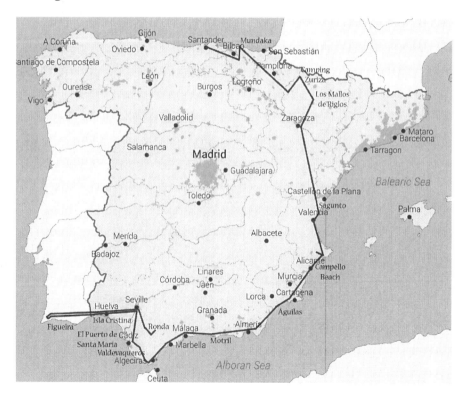

There is a large region of hills forested with cork oaks to the north and west of a line drawn between Algeciras and Ronda and I wanted to have a look at this area. So we drove on some at times very minor roads through Ubrique and Cortes de la Frontera, classic Andalusian white towns and challenging to get through even in our little 'van. The only real problem was the almost complete absence of places to stop. We were in the Parque Natural Sierra de Grazalema and it was heavily fenced off along the road. Visitors seemed to be actively discouraged as indeed they are. Only visitors accompanied by a guide are allowed in apparently. This is a very different approach to that taken by the authorities in the UK but I guess the threats from fire and illegal hunting warrant this sort of restriction.

Eventually we found a *Camino Forrestal* where we could get off. This was a gravel track shown on the map winding into the forest and could be a possible wild camping spot in an area almost devoid of such places but given the heavy rain all morning we didn't risk going very far down it and certainly not off it although I am sure that would be possible in summer. In between showers I got out to take the photograph reproduced below and by the time I had walked just a few yards my shoes were caked with a fine grit bound together by clay. Very sticky and quite hard to clean off as I subsequently discovered.

Cork oaks in the Sierra de Grazalema

This is certainly an area for seeing lots of cork oaks and a little further south from here there is another reserve called *los Alcornocales* which means "cork oaks".

The photograph below shows low cloud after the morning's rain. The village is Atajate just before we joined the main road to Ronda. This whole area is seldom trodden by tourists, most drive straight to Ronda but it is worth exploring assuming you can find somewhere to stop and get out.

Atajate under low cloud

There is not a lot of choice on places to stay with a motorhome at Ronda. We needed a campsite with washing machines and there is only one within walking distance of the town, which was the other necessity. The owners of the site know they have a prime position and charge accordingly.

Ronda is essentially a town of two halves. The old town on the south side of the gorge, which conveniently was the first part we reached as we walked in and on the other side of the gorge the modern town. The lady in the campsite reception waxed lyrical about the new town and how we would enjoy visiting its main street. Which we subsequently did and found it just like any other town high street, full of shops selling things we didn't need.

The gorge between the two is in a sense why this place is a tourist magnet. Probably originally bridged in Roman times the Moors built the first of the bridges which exist today and confusingly it is known as the Roman bridge although it wasn't built by them – the explanation for the name is it may be on the *site* of a Roman bridge. A second, higher bridge, the Old Bridge (17th C), was built next to it and then in the 18th century the spectacular New Bridge was built and it is this extraordinary structure which draws the crowds.

The New Bridge, Ronda

We didn't cross into the new town on our first visit but concentrated on walking the streets of the old town, *La Ciudad* which has more than enough to see though everywhere we looked there was an entrance fee, typically three Euros with the grander sites charging up to four. Skinflints as we are we visited only one site, the old Arabic Baths which I would recommend. There is a video to see which is in Spanish but in CGI it tells the story of old Ronda and how the baths worked, using the Roman idea of a hypocaust to heat the rooms and an ingenious water raising mechanism using a donkey to lift the water up from the river. The picture below shows the Roman bridge, and just beyond it and sunk into the ground are the Arabic baths.

Roman Bridge and Arabic Baths

We finished off our first visit to Ronda with a late lunch at a restaurant with a terrace overlooking a fearsome drop into the gorge.

Despite my best attempt to hide from the Rain Gods by parking under an olive tree at the campsite they found us on the first night. Fortunately, this was followed by a dry morning which allowed us to revisit Ronda.

The rains had done nothing to deter the tour groups, which we found out in force. You could while away a morning here "tour group spotting". This game is played by awarding points for spotting characteristics of tour groups. For example, many of the tour groups were led by people carrying furled umbrellas held aloft. A variation of the game would be to hold your own umbrella aloft to see how long it takes to collect a group of followers, but the umbrella trick was so common it doesn't win many points. The most stylish group leader we saw was a lady carrying aloft instead of an umbrella a full sized real sunflower complete with stem. Ten points for this at least.

Interior of Arabic Baths

The technical class was won by groups led by someone mumbling into a microphone while the group listened in on wireless headphones. At least they were quiet but it deprived us of the chance to earwig in on what was being said and thus miss the chance of finding out about what we were all looking at. I awarded myself a bonus point for spotting the couple in matching see-through plastic raincoats, Dutch or possibly French from the man's moustache.

After the previous days rather expensive but delicious lunch above the gorge we economised on a seven Euro three course menu of the day and good value and tasty it was, even if the pineapple came out of a tin.

Unfortunately, we spent fifteen minutes too long over lunch and were caught in a downpour on the walk back to the site. The photograph below was taken on our walk back and just before our soaking. It shows how Ronda with its natural cliffs was chosen as an easily defended location.

Ronda viewed from the south

I mentioned earlier Ronda was a town of two halves but it is also a town with two very different lives. There is the life involving tourists and then there is the life the locals enjoy which is best seen at the end of the day when virtually all the tourists have departed in their coaches and cars. A good place to see and meet the local people is in the area known as San Francisco, which is on the south edge of Ronda where there is a little plaza. This was very busy when we walked through it with families enjoying the late and prolonged lunches the Spanish are so very good at. The number of people was probably explained by this being a public holiday, Hispanic Day, which commemorates the day when Christopher Columbus first set foot in the Americas in 1492. In the USA this festival is also celebrated where it is known as Columbus Day.

We enjoyed Ronda, despite the crowds but it was time to move as there was one further area I wanted to visit before we started to head back for the ferry. To get there we headed east back along the coast then started some serious climbing up into Las Alpujarras.

The Alpujarras

This is an area I had long wanted to visit after reading Chris Stewart's books in which he described buying a near derelict farmhouse which he subsequently restored by earning money as a sheep shearer. *Driving Over Lemons* is his first and perhaps most famous book but his latest, *End of the Bus Club* I found really enjoyable. Tales of Englishmen who buy old properties in Europe, particularly France and Italy are commonplace. Most of these books are unremarkable but Chris Stewart's books are worth reading as they give an insight into an area and a way of life which many of us know little about. Another good book about the area was written by Gerald Brenan. *South from Granada* describes his time in a remote village, Yegen, where he settled shortly after being demobbed after the First World War. Brenan's book is as much about his state of mind after his time in the trenches as about Spain but it does give some wonderful glimpses of a way of life now long vanished.

The region was first settled and developed by Arabs from North Africa who arrived in the eighth century and employed the farming techniques they had used in the Atlas mountains involving extensive terracing and irrigation systems. The name Alpujarras probably derives from the Arabic for sierra of pastures (*al-bugsharra*).

During the fifteenth century the Arabs were expelled and the Spaniards attempted to take over the slopes, marching large numbers of people down from Galicia to settle them here. However, the incomers were never very successful despite keeping back one or two Arabic families from each village to show them how to work the irrigation systems. The silk industry in particular which had flourished under the previous occupants slowly went downhill although the area today is covered in Mulberry trees in compensation. The Alpujarras remained a depressed and deprived area until new roads began to open it up in the Twentieth Century.

Today the Alpujarras are enjoying slightly better fortunes but unemployment remains high and it is still an area well off the traditional tourist routes – undeservedly so.

There are only a few campsites in the area, including one at Trevélez which claims to be the highest in Spain at around 1550m. As we were to discover the following year this claim is somewhat spurious as it isn't by quite a margin but 1550m is still very high for October so I elected for the slightly lower (1300m) site just outside the village of Pitres. Of course I didn't tell Mary about the altitude but there was no hiding the newly fallen snow we could see on the High Sierras as we wound up the twisty road from the valley floor.

There was some muttering from the ranks when we arrived and got out into single digit temperatures. The phrase "I don't do cold holidays" was distinctly heard. Fortunately, an issue of rum, or to be more accurate, sherry, calmed the mutinous crew member.

It rained during the night, no change there, but we have become used to that but the low cloud all around us when we woke up was new.

Fortunately, by the time we were ready for our walk the sun had burned it off and we had blue skies.

There is a lot of walking done in this region, Chris Stewart runs walking holidays and we saw several groups of walkers in the lower villages on our way up the day before.

We chose a walk called The Seven Villages, which starts in Pitres and over about 3 hours takes you through all the local villages on paths and tracks on one side of the Rio Trevélez valley.

The valley of the Rio Trevélez

The leaflet we had must have been translated from Spanish or possibly French and it was a bit hard to follow at first. For example, the starting point was a path beside a bar in Pitres called, according to the leaflet "La Road" except there wasn't a bar with this name, but there was one called "La Carretela". The leaflet did this a few times, literally translating place names into English, but it did keep us on our toes. The going initially was quite rough as we descended down a rocky path which was probably a torrent during heavy rain.

At one point the printed instructions for the walk said we had to "pass under a large brown" which was intriguing. When we got to the "brown" we discovered it was an ancient and very large sweet chestnut. *Marron* is French for chestnut but it means brown in Spanish. Mystery solved, well almost, because I was sure the walk instructions had been written by an English lady so I suspect the original English had been translated to French then once again into Spanish. No wonder it was as hard going following the instructions as the walking was in places. The picture below shows Mary "scrumping" for sweet chestnuts below the "brown".

Large sweet chestnut

The walk itself was fascinating. This whole area is heavily terraced, much of it abandoned but a huge variety of trees and bushes remain: pomegranate, quince, apple, mulberry, sweet chestnut of course, figs and olives.

The villages we walked through were all contained good examples of the unique architecture of the Alpujarras. The houses, painted white of course, often flow into one another almost organically and they have flat roofs. Originally the roofs were made with flat stones laid on timbers and then sealing the top with clay dug from the river bed. These days it looked as if cement has replaced the clay.

A typical house of the Alpujarras

We finished the walk with lunch in Pitres and a very Spanish dish called *Migres* and very nice it was too. *Migres* is normally made with fried breadcrumbs as it was here though in parts of the Pyrenees they use flour instead. I've eaten both variants and both are delicious.

We were now coming towards the end of our first motorhome trip to Spain so it was time to start thinking about timing our return to the north coast where the weather forecast was looking good for at least until the coming weekend and hopefully into the following week. We had about a week left before we had to catch the ferry so we bade farewell to Las Alpujarras after an all too brief stay.

As we drove down to the valley bottom I stopped a couple of times to take some photographs. This shot shows the villages of Bubión on the right and beyond that Capileira. The highest peak in the Sierra Nevada, Mulhacén, is somewhere beyond the clouds. The second shot shows some *lenticular* clouds, formed by air flowing over the mountains and cooling.

Bubión and Capileira with the High Sierras behind

Big skies and *lenticular* clouds (centre of photograph)

Going Home

Our retreat from the south coast was painless and afforded us an excellent insight into the centre of Spain which probably made us realise for the first time there is a great deal more to Spain than the coast and the mountains.

What you can't avoid driving north from Granada are olives. We drove all day through, around and past olives. The olive is of course an ancient crop, first believed to have been cultivated at least six thousand years ago in the Middle East. The trees can live to a vast age. Radiocarbon dated has shown a number of trees in Malta to be two thousand years old and there are many other claims, though not scientifically proven, of older trees elsewhere in Europe. Some trees in Italy are believed to have been planted in Roman times.

Interestingly, we saw some new plantings where the young olives were very close together in rows. A bit like grapes in a vineyard, possibly for future mechanical harvesting? However, much of the planting was traditional and as we drove we could see slight differences in cultivation practices. Many of the trees were planted in pairs which are usually done with two different cultivars which can cross-pollinate each other. We also saw a few groves where some trees were planted in threes. These latter might also have been signs that the original tree had died off, possibly from a severe frost and the rootstock had regenerated itself, which can happen. The olive is a very hard tree to kill off completely.

Of course the biggest mystery about olives is how did anyone ever discover that you could eat them because when harvested the fruit are completely inedible with a very bitter taste. To make them palatable olives have to undergo a fermentation process to dissolve out the phenolic compound *oleuropein* which is the cause of the bitter taste. There are different ways of fermenting olives but one of the most traditional and widespread is to use a brine solution though probably the best use a process involving natural lactic acid which produces olives which can be stored without the need to be refrigerated after opening.

After our day driving through olives we stopped at a campsite near Santa Elena. The site was called Despeñaperros which is the name of the river which flows through a steep gorge, now a natural park, close to Santa Elena. The gorge has long been used as a passageway for travel from Andalusia to the central plateau of Spain, the *meseta central*. There are Neolithic cave paintings here, the remains of a Roman Road and the website andalucia.com has this to say:

"Despeñaperros has been the site of several fierce battles, the most famous being the Navas de Tolosa battle fought between the fierce Muslim Almohads and the Christians in 1212. It was one of the most decisive battles in the history of Andalucía, since the Christians' overwhelming force paved the way for the reconquest.

Some believe that Despeñaperros was named after this battle, since Despeñaperros could mean the throwing over a cliff (despeñar) of the dogs (perros, or the Moors). For others, the name comes from the cliffs themselves, the despeñaderos."

During the Peninsular War Napoleon had great difficulty maintaining communications and a flow of supplies to Andalusia because the passes here through the Sierra Morena could be held by just a few *guerrilleros*.

The following night, after skirting around the west side of Madrid and then over the Sierra de Guadarrama mountains we stopped virtually in the centre of Valladolid on a car park where several bays had been set aside for motorhomes. It was a short walk from there to the centre of town where we learned to avoid the bars around the *Plaza Mayor*, five Euros for two beers, ouch. We had better value at a bar a short distance away, two tasty and filling tapas and accompanying glasses of a good red wine for eleven Euros for the two of us.

We left early the next morning, we didn't have much choice really, Valladolid like most cities wakes early and the traffic was coming and going before even the sun rose but at least there were no machines going "squeak-aargh". We avoided motorways as much as possible, taking an interesting road northwards from Leon which passed over through the Cantabrica Cordillera mountains, the three hundred kilometre long chain of peaks which runs parallel to the north coast of Spain. This is an extremely deprived area, we saw whole villages virtually deserted and full of houses for sale with only one or two occupied.

The pass at *Pajares* was spectacular, not very high at 1300m but it descends steeply (15% in places) dropping down to join the motorway a little south of Oviedo. This profile is typical of the Cantabrica Cordillera, a gentle climb from the south then a steep descent on the north side. The range marks the divide between the green northern coastal strip and the arid region of central Spain.

We stayed overnight at the fishing port of Navia on a small aire near a supermarket. It wouldn't win any prizes for ambience but it was free which was nice.

Leaving Navia we headed east, initially avoiding the motorway and using the coast road and made the unexpected discovery of a new aire not in our book at Puerto de Vega, another little fishing port. When I say discovered, we saw the blue sign for it but couldn't find it when the road seemed to stop at the port. As I was reversing back out of what I thought was a dead end an old guy signalled for me to go ahead. Not sure if he was having a game of trap the tourist we just waved back but I think he was probably genuine. Subsequent searches using Google maps confirm he was, the aire is a car park beside the port but it isn't visible until you turn a corner after passing the bars. Sadly, it doesn't have any water or waste disposal facilities but it would be pleasant for an overnight stay and an opportunity to mix with the locals.

After this little bit of excitement we returned to the soft embrace of a campsite near the town of Candás a little west of Gijon. We were given a near perfect pitch on the top of the low cliffs above the sea with uninterrupted views north east.

On the way back we had to get Bertie seen by a vet and we stopped at the vets in San Vicente de la Barquera where they spoke excellent English. UK law demands dogs entering from Europe have to be treated for tapeworm and certified fit for travel in addition of course for a rabies vaccination before they leave the UK. The tapeworm treatment is to prevent the introduction into the UK of a specific type of tapeworm (*echinococcus*) which is found in Europe and can cause serious illness in humans.

Boarding the ship at Santander was painless but as always a slow business enlivened only by the discovery of a would-be stowaway under a motorhome just behind us.

The crossing was pretty smooth though it was a bit bouncy at about ten o'clock in the evening but after midnight it was very pleasant. Apparently the ship had had a very rough passage coming out, in the aftermath of a former hurricane and much use of sick bags had been made on board.

The highlights of the trip for us were the Pyrenees, Andalucía generally except the highly populated coastal bits and the north coast. But we also realised there is much to see just about anywhere in Spain including the big flat bits in the middle.

So that concluded our first trip into Spain travelling by motorhome. We came away feeling we had hardly touched the place and we needed to get back there as soon as possible and spend even longer exploring. The following May that is exactly what we did and the account of that trip follows.

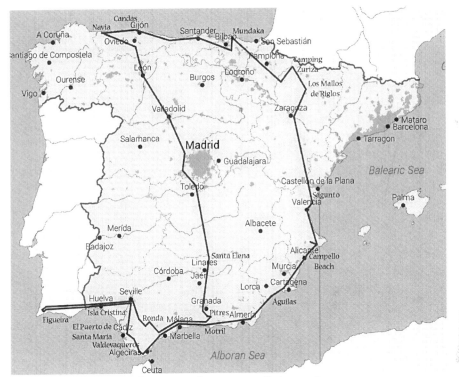

The map of our complete route

Time For Your Last Walkies Bertie

You may have noticed our dog Bertie had a few honourable mentions at the start of this book but then seemed to drop out of sight. This would be a true reflection of how events turned out. Bertie enjoyed the warm weather, he slept most of the time but when awake we began to slowly realise he wasn't really aware at times of what was happening. Things didn't get any better once we got home. The winter wasn't a good time for him and at one point we took him to the vets to ask for their opinion. There are of course no magic pills for old age and the vet told us "we would know when the time came" and we did a few weeks later. In Terry Pratchett's Discworld series Death is a skeletal man and the Death of Rats ("The Grim Squeaker") is a skeletal rat. I don't remember a Death of Dogs character but if there was one it would have been a skeletal dog which came to Bertie one day and told him he was going for his last walkies. This happened just two weeks before our next trip, which is covered in the following section.

The picture below is of Bertie enjoying the warmth of Spain.

Bertie (1998 - 2015)

The Second Journey

Two Go Back to Spain

April to June, 2015

The Ferry to Santander

We live on the outskirts of Plymouth in an area known as the South Hams. The name has nothing to do with bacon but originates from the Old English word "hamme" meaning an enclosed space and is believed here to refer to the mild climate which this sheltered part of South Devon enjoys. This is no coincidence, because it was the climate which brought us here originally. After a working life travelling we had the opportunity as retirement approached to settle down wherever we wanted and South Devon won. We did look elsewhere, Cornwall is attractive but I was still working at the time and it was just a little too far away as was Wales where my wife comes from. I originate from Cumbria which I still love but we wanted somewhere further south with easier travelling into Europe. North Devon, which we also looked at, can be rugged and wild but the softer South Devon was more welcoming and this is where we now live. We have no regrets coming here, it is a wonderful area but we still like to travel and visit new places and South Devon is in a good position for visiting Europe. The south east of England is in a better position if you want the cheapest crossings of the Channel but the south east is alien territory to us, too many folk rushing about in my experience.

Ferries leave Plymouth for France and Spain and we have been over to France several times, landing at Roscoff in Brittany but the longer ferry to Santander we delight in, even if we have had some very rough crossings. One in particular is still remembered vividly. We spent the evening lashed to the bar as the ship ploughed through the huge waves then when we retired to our cabin it was like sleeping in a lift. One moment we were shooting up to the penthouse so to speak and the next crashing down to the basement. We learned on that voyage to avoid cabins near the bows.

Plymouth is famous for ships. It was from here in 1588 Sir Francis Drake, the well-known saviour of England against the Spanish and less well known slaver and pirate was supposed to have left to attack the Spanish navy after finishing his game of bowls. This story is as likely to be true as the uninspiring steps you can see today in Plymouth marked the "Mayflower Steps" actually being the ones down which 102 people descended before sailing to the New World in 1620 to establish the first permanent colony in New England. However, tourism thrives on legends and the South West needs tourists so I certainly won't do anything to puncture these bubbles which draw in the crowds.

On our trip to Spain the previous year we had been accompanied by Bertie, our Jack Russell of great age but the man (or is it a dog?) with the scythe caught up with Bertie just a couple of weeks before we left so it was with a curiously empty but fresher smelling motorhome we started this new trip.

We left towards the end of April, early enough to avoid the peak holiday season but not so early we met the last of the Spanish winter. Although there are parts of the south coast of Spain where you can expect sunshine almost all year, the north coast and interior can be cold and wet, weather which we can stay at home and experience if we want and save ourselves the expense of the ferry, which is considerable.

From a purely financial point of view taking the ferry from Plymouth to Santander in Spain is a bit questionable. We could have taken the shorter and cheaper crossing to Roscoff in Brittany and driven down through France but I don't really like long days of driving and western France in April is not well known for its warmth and reliable sunshine, so trying to make the journey part of the holiday is an uphill struggle at that time of year. There are folk who make getting to the south of Spain in the shortest possible time almost an obsession and I have read magazine articles discussing the best and quickest routes from the channel ports to the bottom of Spain. This is not for me. Having the luxury of choice I take the short drive to Plymouth Docks, spend a little under a day on the ferry and then drive off into Spain. As I mentioned in the first part of this book it is really a little like flying somewhere for a holiday, you leave home, queue up for a while, embark and after a few hours reading, eating and drinking you step off in a completely different place to where you started from. The big difference with flying is you leave most of your luggage in your vehicle so there is little chance of it getting lost and your bags going off on a holiday of their own.

First of course, we actually had to *leave* home, hopefully safely and without incident. Our house is in a narrow Devon lane and I have to reverse our motorhome into this lane, passing between a pair of solid stone gateposts as we do so. I now know one of these stone structures quite well because after last year's trip of just under three thousand incident free miles around Spain we came home from the ferry and I collided with the gatepost, leaving me with an expensive repair bill.

Fortunately, this year's departure turned out better than last year's return, in terms of damage to vehicle and garden fittings, so we arrived at the Brittany Ferries' terminal with a vehicle looking ready for a holiday and not a trip to the body shop.

Boarding a ferry is a slow process but the ferry operators have a cunning trick to make it seem as if something is happening when it isn't. What they do is to move you along every now and again, which gives an impression of progress even though the exercise does nothing for reducing the actual time it is going to take to board. So first you queue up to show your ticket, get directed to a numbered lane where you sit and wait, watching the other lanes move off and wondering when it will be your turn. Then when it *is* your turn to move you are just directed to another numbered lane a little further on where you wait a bit more. This process of creeping up to the ferry in stages needs to be taken in good spirit. You are after all going on your holidays and must at all costs avoid getting upset. Especially when they tease you as they did with us this time, bringing us forward until we were *almost* at the ramp, then pulling us to one side and waving on other vehicles instead, while we watched helplessly as they drove past us. Not that there is really much point getting on as early as possible as sometimes getting on near the end means you are one of the first to get off at the destination and of course we did have a ticket and they weren't going to leave us behind. Or so we hoped because no doubt there is something in the fine print, a bit like airlines, which means you are not guaranteed a place even if you have a valid ticket.

Finally, we were ushered onto the ferry, which I entered while trying to avoid hitting any French seaman as we drove slowly over the various chains, lumps and bumps which littered the vehicle deck. A recent innovation on this route is there is a member of the crew waiting to hand you a card which shows where the nearest set of stairs are and much more importantly acts as a reminder to help you *find* your vehicle at the end of the voyage. Being someone who regularly loses their car in multi-story car parks I find this little card very useful.

We made our way on foot up umpteen decks and found our cabin after only getting lost a few times. There is no doubt a French logic to how the cabins are numbered and the decks designed but it escapes me and on this voyage I was never to reach our cabin by the same route twice. It is possible the cabins actually *move* and the whole thing is a Gallic joke on the English. Nothing would surprise me.

After dropping off our overnight bags we made directly for the best place on the ship – the Piano Bar, so called because as you might guess it has a piano and sometimes someone to play it as well. The bar also has big windows out of which we watched the last of the evening sunshine while we drank a glass of wine or two.

The ferry was the *Pont Aven* which Brittany Ferries call their flagship although they have recently placed an order for a new vessel which will replace it as the largest of their fleet. This new vessel is to be called the *Honfleur* and is named after a pretty port in Normandy.

As we like to pamper ourselves on this ferry, treating it as a mini-cruise, we booked a table in the *Flora* restaurant, or the "posh restaurant" as it is sometime known as. There is a normal self-service place you can use, and most do, as being a French ship with French chefs they do serve food a cut above motorway services standard.

Inevitably, our meal was expensive and was the joint most expensive meal we were to eat on the entire trip, being only equalled by the cost of the meal we ate on the same ship on the return leg.

Formal entertainment is lacking in the *Flora* restaurant although we could faintly hear the piano player in the bar next door, but there is no end of opportunity for people watching, with all the entertainment this sport can produce. The first thing I do is to identify the miserable people, those with down-turned mouths or faces like the proverbial smacked bottom to use a cliché. They are always some around sitting grumpily moaning about everything or just sitting and brooding in silence. Then there are the "plate-pilers" who go to the buffet and help themselves to a little bit of everything and return cautiously carrying a plate on which a huge cone of food is piled. Depressingly, many of these folk actually eat it all and then go back for more. You can feel the ship rolling as they walk from one side of the deck to another. Then there are those who clearly don't like sharing the restaurant with the likes of us. These ones usually go for the *a la carte* menu where the staff bring the dishes to their table which they eat without looking around in case they catch the eye of a commoner.

After dinner we sat in the Piano Bar for a while then went off to our cabin, which had clearly moved as we could only find it by taking a different route to the one we had used to find it earlier.

It is very spooky how they move the cabins around without anyone noticing.

The weather is always a concern when you are on a ship, or it is to a bad sailor like me. During the day of departure it had been very windy in Plymouth so I was expecting the worst but as the ship sailed past the Plymouth breakwater we found the sea outside was remarkably calm. There was a bit of rolling and bumping at first (late diners moving around perhaps) but around midnight even this stopped and we had and even enjoyed a very calm crossing.

We woke to find that we were surrounded by a sea which looked almost oily it was so smooth and given the amount of pollution in our seas this observation may not be far from the truth.

We made our way to the restaurant for breakfast and were lucky enough to get a window seat, which even though the window was a bit dirty on the outside (they always are) gave us a good view over the silky water. Breakfast is a help yourself buffet, so we helped ourselves and took our time over eating it.

The Plymouth to Santander ferry is famous for whale and dolphin watching, which is at its best as the vessel crosses the Bay of Biscay and sails beyond the continental shelf into much deeper waters. The depth here is over three thousand meters although curiously, unlike on an aircraft the captain does not announce this fact. On an aircraft they always say how high and fast you are flying but on a ship an announcement like this is never heard, perhaps panic might ensue if it did: "Ladies and Gentlemen, we are travelling at twenty four knots and have over three kilometres of deep dark water below us." You can easily imagine the ensuing rush for the lifeboats and the folk pulling up short when they realise the lifeboats are just going to put them over three kilometres of deep dark water in a less seaworthy vessel than the one they are on already.

Although the Bay of Biscay is the best place for the big whales, dolphins and porpoises can be seen close to Plymouth and one year as our ferry approached Roscoff on the north coast of France we were preceded by a large pod of dolphins leaping ahead of us for a few moments before they veered away. The Bay of Biscay hotspot is along the continental shelf where there is a region of sloping sea bed between the shallower continental shelf and the deep waters of the ocean proper. Here the rich water offers the best feeding opportunities for the whales. An upwelling of nutrient rich water from the deep ocean is fed upon by phytoplankton which begins a food chain which ends with the whales. In particular there are two canyons, called the Santander and Torrelavega canyons which run towards the coast and are perfectly positioned for extended whale watching from ferries sailing into Santander and Bilbao.

Although whales *are* seen from these vessels it doesn't mean you *will* see anything. Dolphins are not unusual and I have seen them several times. They are a great spirit lifter, leaping and screaming through the waves wearing a "look at me I'm a dolphin" expression. Big whales are by no means common and a sighting is a rarity. I've sailed a few times on this route before and the best we have seen was a solitary Minke Whale, which isn't quite a fully paid up member of the

Really Big Whales Club but at a usual size of six to eight metres is no minnow either, so it did count as a Notable Sighting.

Fortunately, this morning saw a turn in our luck though the signs for good whale watching were not good as the ferry seemed to sailing through fog first thing in the morning but as the sun rose the fog or sea mist started to clear and visibility improved considerably.

The first sightings were a group of what I took initially to be dolphins. We saw them from the restaurant while we were having breakfast from our treasured window seat. Though I thought they must be dolphins they didn't look quite right as they were breaking the water surface, which was very calm, with a sort of rolling motion, a bit like a porpoise does but they were considerably bigger than porpoises, which are the smallest of the *cetaceans* you are likely to see. There were quite a few of them in the pod, well over twenty, with very prominent dorsal fins and we watched them closely as they disappeared into the remains of the mist.

After breakfast we decided to go for a walk on the deck and while trying to reach the upper deck we discovered there was a talk on whales being given. We hadn't heard any announcements about this otherwise we would have gone to it, which as things turned out would have been unfortunate. Not wishing to disturb the talk by barging in halfway through we went out onto the deck and started a slow circuit around the ship. At one point we came across two ladies pointing out to sea, where we spotted a couple of very large and very dark shapes low in the water and some distance away. Their shape was very distinctive, very flat along the top on which there was only the hint of a small, triangular shaped bump and a very blunt nose. Then suddenly there was a puff of spray, which formed a roughly circular cloud in the air and a few moments later one after another they lifted up their great tail fins or flukes high in the air and then slipped down into the depths. I was a bit stunned, I had a suspicion what they might be but I wasn't confident enough to voice it. Of course not expecting to see any whales this early in the year my camera and telephone lens were safely locked in our cabin.

A little later in the morning I spoke with the two resident whale watchers from the ORCA charity who had been giving the talk we had managed to miss. I described our breakfast sighting, which they said were Pilot Whales and then our sightings of the two large whales, which they unhesitatingly said from my description could only have been Sperm Whales, which are only sighted a few times a year.

Dolphins also put in an appearance a couple of times during the day, the smaller and brightly coloured Common Dolphin although other species, particularly Bottlenose are also regularly seen on this route.

Three *cetacean* species seen in one morning, the trip couldn't have got off to a better start.

Arrival

The first glimpse of Spain from the ferry is one of mountains. The Picos de Europa could be distantly glimpsed far to the east, covered in snow this early in the year, but the land immediately behind Santander is also very mountainous. The Picos are of course the best known mountains of northern Spain, the name translates as the "Peaks of Europe" and the widespread belief is the name arose because these were the first mountains of Europe mariners saw when returning from the New World. It sounds plausible until you wonder what route the sailors might have been taking for the Picos to be their first sighting of land. Even if they were heading for Santander or one of the ports further to the east, such as Bilbao, would they not have seen the cliffs of Galicia first? It is a small mystery without a clear answer although the popular explanation is well established and may well be true, even if it was only called the Picos de Europa by mariners with a poor sense of direction.

Arrival in Santander is a slightly drawn out affair as you need to pass several headlands and offshore islands before your ship finally turns into the sheltered Bay of Santander. Sitting in our usual seats in the Piano Bar we waited for the call to go down to the car deck, which was eventually heard and after only a little confusion while we hunted for the correct stairway we were back in our vehicle and waiting for unloading to start, which as always seemed to take forever but eventually the vehicles in front of us began to move and we drove out into the Spanish sunshine of the early afternoon. I had already loaded into the satnav the coordinates of our first overnight stopover, so after a perfunctory inspection of our passports we were waved off and let loose on the motorways and dual carriageways which surround Santander.

Having been thwarted the previous year from visiting Galicia by the Rain Gods we were determined to go there this year whatever the weather threw at us. Fortunately, our resolve wasn't going to be severely tested too early in the trip as the forecast for the next few days looked good, but we were going to take things steadily so our first night was spent barely twenty kilometres from Santander at a wildlife park among the little hills which lie inland from the port.

The Cabárceno Wildlife Park is a set in a former opencast iron ore mine, iron having once been a major export of the region and the UK a major customer in the nineteenth century. Today, the former mine and some of the surrounding hillsides have been turned into a Spanish Longleat with elephants and other exotic animals wandering freely. An extensive parking area beside the lake is open to the public and this has become well known in the motorhome community as somewhere to stay after arriving from or waiting to board the ferry to Plymouth or Portsmouth. This type of facility is generally known in the motorhoming community as an aire. Which is a French word in which language they are more formally known as "aire de service camping cars" though they are never referred to as an aire by any sign beside the road, usually just by the symbol for a motorhome. Aires have been established in profusion by many small French towns and villages to attract motorhomes in an effort to encourage visitors to spend money in the community and other European countries have copied their example. The only country which has noticeably not copied the French is the UK which as a generality remains distinctly motorhome unfriendly compared to the rest of western Europe.

Despite their popularity in Europe, aires were a new experience to us but we were rapidly growing to appreciate them. Not least because many of them are free which is a great attraction even if some aires, and we were to stay in one or two of them in the forthcoming weeks, can be in pretty unattractive locations, but when it isn't costing you anything for a night's accommodation the surroundings can seem less important. Of course Cabárceno *is* in an attractive setting, surrounded by rocky hills as seen in the photograph below and after we had arrived we took a gentle walk along the boundary fence to the park and watched the elephants grazing on the grass.

Some aires are just car parks without any facilities for getting fresh water or discharging waste water but the Cabárceno aire does have these facilities although they are remarkably grim and dirty, which does somewhat reduce the attraction of this location but if like us and you didn't need to take on fresh water having arrived with full tanks, the place is perfect. There is even a bar in the little village a short walk away which we visited in the early evening for a cold beer.

There were quite a few British motorhomes already here when we arrived, the two nearest us were owned by couples on their way back to the UK having over-wintered in Spain. These hardy souls were having a BBQ in the weak evening sun but we huddled inside and had a curry which we had packed frozen in the refrigerator before setting off. We were not yet quite in the full holiday spirit.

Over-wintering in Spain is very popular amongst European motorhomers, not just the British but Dutch, Germans and French can be found in huge numbers all along the southern coast of Spain and around into southern Portugal. Sometimes groups of hundreds of vehicles can gather in one seaside town, often parking on waste ground or car parks. Local bars and restaurants welcome their custom but many residents don't.

The aire at Cabárceno

The French have traditionally gone in large numbers beyond Spain into Morocco, where the French language is still quite widely spoken but recent events in the Islamic world have made this a less popular destination. Of course you don't need a motorhome to overwinter somewhere. We were later to meet a couple who even though they *had* a motorhome they chose to rent an apartment in Goa for the winter, saying it was cheaper to live there than in Spain and considerably warmer.

After a good night's sleep it would be nice to say we were woken the following morning by the distant trumpeting of elephants, but it was to the sound of a digger noisily moving large rocks around that roused us into consciousness on our first full day in Spain.

Yet despite the plumbing and the early morning sound effects, Cabárceno is an excellent overnight halt but do bring your own water. I have subsequently heard the water which gurgles out of a sort of faucet there is safe to drink but I suggest avoid it unless desperate.

The Adventure Begins

Our first full day is Spain started with us doing the touristy thing and visiting Santillana del Mar, which is frequently called Spain's prettiest village, most frequently by those owning businesses there. Though undeniably attractive, it isn't unique and Albarracín, which we were to visit towards the end of our trip, was on a very different level. However, Santillana del Mar got its "prettiest" description from the Nobel Prize winning author John-Paul Sartre and inevitably his opinion carries a degree of clout and the reputation has stuck, although he did make this comment "*le plus joli village d'Espagne*" in a novel which is a thing made up and of the imagination.

But first we needed to stock up the cupboards so we headed for Torrelavega, a large and busy town a little to the west of Santander which has a cluster of easily reached supermarkets close to the motorway. Offshore, the Torrelavega canyon is where the large whales come to feed and onshore we had learned on the grapevine this is where motorhomers come to find food. Naturally, we headed directly for the Lidl supermarket, which we knew from experience would have all our simple tastes required. Outside the supermarket we found beside the shopping trolleys the same man we had seen on our visit the previous year, collecting spare change from the shoppers. We were subsequently to discover that every Lidl store in Spain has exactly one person standing outside doing this but they were rarely seen outside other supermarkets. Perhaps Lidl were running some sort of apprenticeship scheme. If so, it was working because I gave the man another Euro to go with the one he got from me last year.

Santillana del Mar gets the first part of its name from St Juliana (or Santa Illana - they really are bad at spelling these Spaniards) whose remains are in the Collegiate church, a former Benedictine monastery. The second part of the name is equally perplexing as the town is some distance from the sea although the local authorities seem to have recognised this as all the signposts pointing to the place just say Santillana with not a "Mar" in site.

This did confuse us when we arrived because at first we couldn't see any of the fabled buildings and the place was so quiet there was no one to follow. Were we in the wrong Santillana; is there another one with a more salty air? Fortunately, we were saved by the arrival of a coach load of French school children who did seem to know where to go and we certainly were not too proud to follow them as they strode off purposefully. For anyone else who arrives in the same state of ignorance as us the old bits, coming from Torrelavega, are on the right hand side of the main road.

It took us an hour or so to explore and take photographs, virtually every house in the village seemed to have been converted into a shop selling leather wallets but the streets were undeniably attractive and we probably should have spent longer there but this early in the trip our feet were itching to move and so we left without even having a cup of coffee.

Santillana del Mar

We stopped for our second night in Spain at the end of the coastal road beyond Muros de Nalón at San Esteban at the mouth of the river Nalón, in the province of Asturias. At the end of this road was a single restaurant beside which we parked and a very long quay which was completely deserted of any shipping. We walked the full length of this quay, passing sections where the sea was reclaiming it and wondered whose idea it had been to build it because clearly as a maritime venture it was a complete and sad failure.

Along the North Coast

The restaurant near where we were parked closed early if it even ever opened as we didn't see any customers while we were there, so we had a quiet night until we were woken by the distant sounds of aircraft taking off from Gijon airport from about seven in the morning. Gijon is the major port of Asturias, a province like several others in Spain which has its own unique language, in which the city is spelt Xixon and pronounced something like "Heekon" but with a guttural, throat clearing inflection in the middle of the word. Signposts in this area show alternative spellings for many place names and naturally the activists have been out with their aerosol cans ensuring linguistic pollution is prevented and the accepted Spanish spellings are obliterated. It is ironic that a province which by name is plural does not seem to tolerate plural spelling.

Fortunately, our satnav doesn't know how to read signposts in any language so it was unfazed by the impromptu redecoration and it took us unhesitatingly along the coast to Puerto de Vega, a pretty little port where we believed it might be possible to stay by the harbour. The harbour is reached after you have driven past a row of harbour side bars, which was certainly encouraging but when we came to the harbour itself we found workman using pneumatic drills as part of a project to repair the seawall.

It might have made a pleasant overnight stop but the air was full of dust and noise so we left the little harbour by the road marked "*todas directions*" at the back of the car park, which seemed reasonable as the way we had arrived was quite narrow but this turned out to be a mistake. The road started at an inviting gradient then became steeper and narrow. We eventually escaped without too much trouble or under body scraping but Puerto de Vega will have to wait until another year when the harbour repairs are complete but if we do visit again we will certainly leave by the bar-strewn harbour approach road and keep well away from *todas directions*.

Our westward journey so far had been along a mixture of coastal roads and the impressive north coast motorway, an extraordinary example of civil engineering which successively tunnels through mountains and then vaults over wide valleys on viaducts each individually identified by a sign giving the name of the river below and the precise length of the viaduct to the exact metre.

The motorway is a quick way to travel but of course like all motorways they are not the best way to see a country, for which you need to get off the motorway and travel on minor roads.

The sunshine which had greeted us as we arrived in Spain had by now exhausted itself and the weather had turned to intermittent drizzle, which was more the sort of thing experience has taught us to expect along the north coast of Spain. So without much reason to linger we pushed on west, leaving Asturias we came to a halt just inside Galicia at a campsite close to the town of Foz, a former whaling port.

Galicia occupies Spain's north western corner and is a region famed for its seafood and seafaring. It is also supposed to be the greenest part of Spain though from personal experience I am fairly sure the north coast further west can offer very good competition in the rain stakes. The coastline is rocky and is characterized by rias, which are flooded river valleys. To the untutored eye, which before I came to live near a ria in Devon certainly described me, a ria is just somewhere where a river flows into the sea and the feature might be called an estuary, but a ria characteristically has steep sides and here in Galicia they were formed when the land sunk and the sea flowed up the river valleys after the glaciers which had made them melted, a melting which in turn caused the sea to rise and flood the new valleys still further. More definitively a ria does not need a major river flowing into it either, which happens where the entire former valley has been flooded.

Foz is the first ria you encounter as you enter Galicia from the west but the Ria de Foz is not the most striking of rias as the land either side of the Rio Masma (this is a ria with a river just to add confusion) has a decidedly estuarine appearance, but I won't argue with the geographers and a ria it is named and so it shall remain.

We chose a campsite as we wanted to spend a couple of nights here and catch up with the laundry, a task around which much ingenuity has been applied by campers down the years. For example, if you know you are going to be driving for a day then putting the clothes in a plastic box with a tightly fitting lid works very well, the motion of the vehicle giving the water some vigorous agitation. A salad spinner also makes a useful spin dryer even if it can't take more than a couple of pairs of socks or one shirt at a time. Give it a good rinse out afterwards before using it for lettuce of course. However, buying a few tokens from the campsite office and using the proper facilities is very convenient and when the time comes for washing sheets and duvet covers more or less essential for us. There are of course launderettes but searching them out and finding somewhere to park the vehicle close to them is not something we have felt much urgency to do. In France, where they are more organised about these things, they have outdoor washing machines and tumble dryers at some of the larger supermarkets. These are a very useful thing to find when the sheets are beginning to move of their own accord.

The site we were on was just behind some low cliffs above a long beach. The cliff has been eroded in many places leaving isolated squat stacks which jutted up out of the sand. A little further east from where we were was the *Playa de los Catedrales* where there are further low stacks and rock arches which are popularly supposed to look like the flying buttresses of a cathedral, although the original name for the beach was *Praia de Augas Santas* or Beach of the Holy Waters which suggests nothing to do with rock formations. Perhaps the earlier name was good for attracting pilgrims but when that trade diminished they tried a rebranding?

The beach and coastline near Ribadeo

Along the top of the cliffs and between the drop and the road ran a well paved and quite new path. This path was slightly curious because it hugged the cliff top even when there were houses built on it. In every case but one the path squeezed through the gap between the cliff top and the bottom of the garden except for one house where the path detoured round the front of it. Was this the house of the local mayor who didn't want folk walking past his view? We never found out but it was the only one which hadn't lost the bottom of its garden to the new path.

The path ran amongst carpets of flowers of largely unidentifiable species because to save space and weight I hadn't brought a flower book with me and regretted this on the first walk we took. This was spring and lots of plants were in bloom everywhere but I struggled to put a name to many of them, but one that was easy to spot as it was so striking in flower and was very common was Hottentot Fig (*Carpobrotus edulis*) a native of South Africa which has become an invasive pest in many parts of the world. As its name suggests it is edible, both leaves and flowers apparently, but we had already shopped for supper so gave it a miss. The leaves hold a huge mass of water and the weight of the plant as it grows can build up to a point when the whole plant slides away on steep sandy slopes dragging much of the sand it is growing on with it. The flowers of the fig were impressive though.

Hottentot fig flower

The next day brought much better weather with sunshine and virtually no wind. In the morning we went for another walk, turning left this time outside the campsite and following the footpath in the opposite direction to the way we had taken the previous day. After a while we took some steps down onto the beach and walked along the tideline, where gentle waves were lapping, to the little sandy point which juts out where the Rio Masma flows into the sea at the Ria de Foz. A short distance across the river we could see Foz itself, which looked an attractive town in the sunshine.

Foz looking over the Rio Masma

We then turned inland and walked up the river bank which was topped with large flat stones. We could see shoals of mullet were feeding in the shallows, easily visible in the clear water. The tide was ebbing and the current flowing out to sea was considerable. This was not a place to fall in if you didn't want to be carried quickly out into the bay.

On returning to the campsite we noticed an excellent wild camping spot, with hard standing and its own set of toilets and taps just opposite the campsite entrance. Wild camping is the term used by motorhomers to describe a stopping place they can use overnight where there is otherwise no designated parking for motorhomes. For example, it could be a disused factory, some waste ground or a forest track and locations can vary from the truly wild such as the one we used later in our trip when we stopped in the Corozal forest, to some positively urban locations. The practice is controversial especially where motorhomes gather on residential streets as sometimes happens at popular seaside locations. In the UK, with the exception of some parts of Scotland, there is always the risk of a late night knock by the police and a polite but firm request to move on. In much of Europe there is greater tolerance but parking outside the gates of a campsite did seem to be pushing the envelope a bit but the next morning we found a British motorhome parked there which seemed to have been left in peace by the campsite owner.

On our last evening at the site, after a cold beer or two in the camp bar we gave our new gas BBQ its first outing, cooking some chicken thighs. A cut of meat which is strangely hard to find in Spain where they seem to dine exclusively on wings, whole legs or skinless breasts with not a glimpse of a thigh.

We have tried many different BBQs down the years and the subject of the perfect motorhome BBQ divides opinion. There is no doubt a classic kettle BBQ burning charcoal gives the only true authentic BBQ flavour to the food but they are messy to store and clean out afterwards if you have to carry them around in a motorhome. So after some deliberation, including a trial with a very cheap Chinese gas BBQ, which was remarkably effective at reducing even the best meat to charred remains in a matter of moments we have settled on a small folding gas BBQ. To be honest this is just a gas powered hot plate in that the food whilst above the flames does not actually see them as there is an enamelled metal plate in the way, but it does work and is much easier to clean out than a charcoal BBQ and there is no hot ash to dispose of afterwards. Motorhomers do have to compromise some times and the lack of a true BBQ is one of them but the gas version is a reasonable substitute and campsite rules usually prohibit the use of charcoal burning BBQs because of the fire risk from the ashes and sparks, especially in the hotter and drier parts of southern Europe.

Lugo

Leaving the campsite we headed briefly east, back the way we had arrived, to Ribadeo, a town which lacked a Lidl supermarket but it did have an Eroski, a sort of Spanish Co-Op jointly owned by the employees and customers, which with over a thousand outlets in the country are found almost everywhere. Apart from the usual food we also bought several more "bricks" which is the common name used in Spain for one litre cartons of wine which are usually priced well under a Euro a litre, possibly making the wine cheaper than bottled water and certainly cheaper than diesel. The Eroski ones were not as cheap as the Lidl bricks but at the equivalent of about sixty pence for a carton it was still a remarkably low price. It is hard to imagine the producers making much profit from this stuff but we have found if well chilled, whatever its colour, red, white or pink, it is a pleasant drink and with an alcohol content of typically around eleven percent it is perhaps a little friendlier to the liver than many bottled wines.

Our destination was the city of Lugo which has some very old walls dating back to the Roman period and unlike the Roman road of the Sierra de Gredos which we were to come across later I knew in advance the walls were there. This does prove that a little research before leaving on a trip does pay off, though a little more research might have thrown up the Roman road of the Sierra de Gredos.

After our shopping we drove south, away from the coast, climbing through mixed pine and eucalyptus forests for a couple of hours. Eucalyptus is not native to Europe but it has been widely planted as a source of timber, frequently, and controversially, replacing native oak. With few if any European insects or animals able to eat its leaves and its ability to suppress other plants from growing near it due to the chemicals it releases, a trick known as allelopathy, the plant flourishes wherever it is planted, providing there is enough water to meet its copious demands.

During our drive through the eucalyptus we encountering a large cycle race coming towards us escorted by police motorcyclists. The cyclists were on a downhill stretch and moving very quickly, the motorcycle escort ushering us and other traffic away as they descended. The Spanish are as keen as the French on their cycling and this event just looked like a local club race as some of the back markers looked about my age, but the local police had still turned out to escort them over the mountains.

As we had throughout the trip we used a combination of maps, road atlas and satnav (aka GPS) to find our route to Lugo. The satnav is certainly convenient but you need to keep an eye on it as ours has a tendency to occasionally take some routes which can be best described as "scenic" if not "downright eccentric". A favourite trick it has is to take a short cut off a major road along a narrow track or something equally unsuitable for making good progress. No amount of fiddling in the settings seems to curb this trait and we have grown used to it and can recognise the symptoms and take avoiding action. It does sometimes take us to and through places which we wouldn't have seen otherwise, what I call "satnav tourism" and we have discovered some little gems by this method, so it is not wholly to be decried.

Of course, whether you should be using a satnav at all is something worth considering. They have become almost ubiquitous and many wouldn't consider a journey across Europe without one but it is worth considering what you might be missing by using a GPS and I speak as one of the guilty ones. The biggest disadvantage of them is that by definition, in order to use one you have to tell it your destination, from which it works out using its clever little algorithms a route there and off you subsequently go, listening to the verbal directions or in my case glancing at the screen as I invariably have the sound turned off. The problem is your day can all too easily become a period spent following directions to where you want to go and this means driving past or near all sorts of interesting places which you would enjoy if you just stopped. However, to stop or turn away from the GPS-dictated route and most importantly the GPS-dictated *timetable*, which you have already taken into account when choosing the destination and have mentally prepared yourself for, takes will power. It is all too easy to fall into the trap of driving if not quite in a tunnel, because you can see the countryside you are driving through, but it is as if you are in the bottom a steep sided valley. You can see the mountains around you and the towns you drive through but stop? Stopping means you will be late but late for what as your destination was chosen by you? A much braver technique is to start each day with no clear idea where you are going other than a general idea of "keeping the sea on my right" but I confess we have not quite reached that elevated state of relaxed travelling. It is perhaps telling that in Buddhism freedom from restlessness is only achieved when you reach the very highest of the four stages of enlightenment, having shed such evils as ill will to others and sensual desire on the way, so I don't feel too bad that my itchy feet tend to keep me moving as I'm not ready to discard the latter yet. We did eventually find much later on this trip we could turn away from the satnav chosen path from time to time and not feel guilty. This level of satnav enlightenment is indeed a state to be savoured if it can be achieved.

On this occasion, slavishly following its electronic dictation, the GPS took us through the streets of Lugo, throwing in a quick preview tour of the walls just in case we hadn't planned to visit them or even knew they were there, and without mishap we arrived at a large car park with equally large bays for motorhomes on the south west side of the city overlooking the river. This exercise was a very good example of where a satnav can be invaluable, which is not to say we couldn't have found where we were going by following the printed instructions but the satnav adds useful little snippets such as "keep in the right hand lane", which written instructions rarely do.

The park we arrived at is a listed aire and can be used by motorhomes for overnight parking, having a service point for taking on fresh water and disposing of all manner of liquid and not so liquid wastes. It is hard to think of anywhere in the UK where they would build such a facility close to a city centre if they even built one at all. If this vehicle park was in the UK it would probably have height barriers on the entrance and a machine to take your money for the privilege of staying there. This park had no barriers and no ticket machine.

From the car park it was a fairly short but steeply uphill walk to the city centre. Lugo is the only city in the world to have a complete Roman wall surrounding it, although inevitably the wall has been "improved" in places during the intervening centuries. A wide, gravelled walkway runs along the top of the wall for its entire two and a half kilometre length. We strolled around this, looking down into the city centre and outwards where we could because despite this being a major historical site you wouldn't think so because the city has been built right up to the foundations of the wall which makes it very hard to get a good look at the structure. Most of the time your view of the wall is only of a path stretching away between high buildings which look down onto this Third Century and UNESCO World Heritage Site. Of course to display the walls properly would require the demolition of much of the modern city, an action which the City Fathers seem reluctant to take for some reason.

Lugo is built in a typical defensive position on a hill overlooking the River Minho, a river we were to come across again near the end of our visit to Galicia. An old bridge crosses the river below where we were parked. It looks Roman but only the foundations of three of the pillars are of Roman origin a fact only discovered when the river was diverted for the building of a sewer a few years ago. Lugo is named after the Celtic god Lugos, the god of light, oaths and the arts but gentle Lugos was no defence against the Romans who conquered it in

13 BC and renamed it *Lucus Augusti* making it a military camp and the centre of an active gold mining region, the mineral which probably first drew the Romans to this region.

The walls of Lugo. The inner city on the left

Lugo is very much worth a visit, we were there in desultory drizzle but the wall is worth a circuit even if its impact is muted by the closeness of modern buildings. Before we left our car park overlooking the river I went over to speak to another motorhome which was UK registered and had some stickers on it which I thought I recognised. When I got closer I realised my eyes were not playing tricks, this was a couple who sell amongst other things guides to the aires of several European countries and they were on a visit to Spain to update the current guide for the next edition. We had a chat for a few minutes, during which I let drop I had a copy of their book, but I steered the conversation away from how we had actually arrived, which was using GPS coordinates gleaned from a free online website of aires and campsites.

Lugo to A Coruña

Lugo is inland Galicia and visiting it meant a bit of a detour away from the coast but we corrected this by heading from Lugo to A Coruña, Galicia's second city and its former capital. A Coruña is an old port and it was here that that most famous of Romans Julius Caesar landed some fifty years before the fall of Lugo to start the trade in metals, an activity which soon saw commerce going on with what are now the countries of France, England and Portugal.

We had come to A Coruña to see the Torre de Hercules lighthouse, whose claim to fame is being the oldest lighthouse to have been in continuous operation anywhere in the world. The current name is a relatively recent change, until the Twentieth Century it was known as the *Farum Brigantium*. The word farum is Greek in origin and a lighthouse in Spanish today is still called a faro just as in France they are phares. It is only us prosaic and literal English who eschew this romantic term and call them lighthouses.

The *Hercules* in the name used today stems from the legend that on this site Hercules slew the giant Geryon and buried his head where the lighthouse now stands and ordered a city to be built around it. It may be legend but the city makes the most of it and the coat of arms of A Coruña depicts the lighthouse in the centre with skull and crossbones below it. Unfortunately, the generally accepted version of the Tenth Labour of Hercules has him slaying Geryon much further south, though the exact location depends on deciding where to put the pin in the map for the fabled land of Erytheia. However, there is no doubting that today an impressive lighthouse sits on a rocky peninsula and when you visit it you can see some of the Second Century stones on which it is built, possible on foundations of Phoenician origin but evidence for that seems only slightly less scanty than the evidence Hercules was here once burying the head of a giant. A giant who in some accounts may have had three heads, which must have given Hercules another labour, digging a hole in the solid rock large enough to receive them all.

Our GPS had the coordinates of a car park near the lighthouse on which you are allowed to stay overnight. On arrival this turned out to be the car park for the aquarium and it was very busy with buses full of Spanish school kids and much toing and froing of people. We may indeed have been able to stay there but it was close to a busy road and a relaxed night of sleep seemed unlikely.

We parked up anyway and walked the short distance to the lighthouse, past the aquarium, which has an outside pool of seawater in which we could see some seals swimming around. The lighthouse is built on a rocky little hill and around it was dotted various bits of modern sculpture. Or rather I took them to be modern sculpture as opposed to just some very bad attempts at modelling figures in stone and steel.

The Torre de Hercules with sculpture

The lighthouse was extensively rebuilt in the eighteenth century and only a few stones remain from the Roman structure, which can be seen in the foundations in the little exhibition you walk into after paying your three Euro entrance fee.

From the ground to just below the light the tower is square, a cross section which seems untraditional for a lighthouse but this one is well above the waves so does not need the wave defeating shape of a Smeaton tower. Only the very top of the tower is circular. The stairs from the bottom follow the inside of the walls, creating a square spiral staircase which is just visible on the outside walls. Rooms are found at various points where you can catch your breath and the views – which if I can wander off topic for a moment is a zeugma, which is where one word serves two functions. Famous examples are "She left the ball in a temper and a sedan chair" and from Star Trek; "You are free to execute your laws and your citizens." I only know this linguistic gem from reading Edward Enfield's Greece on my Wheels, a book which I strongly recommend even if you have no interest in cycling. It is a great travel book which will tell you next to nothing about cycling but a lot about Lord Byron's adventures in Greece.

Closer view of the lighthouse

The last section of the ascent from the room at the top of the square stairs is a classic circular spiral staircase, quite narrow, which makes for fun when you meet someone coming down as you are trying to go up. Curiously, or perhaps not, the staircase goes the wrong way round compared to those found traditionally in castles. The established wisdom for spiral staircases dictates that from the bottom they should curve upwards and to the right, forming what in the engineering world would be called a left handed thread. The theory is this puts a defender at the advantage as it gives them more room to wield their sword, assuming of course they are right handed. This may explain why the A Coruña lighthouse has a right handed spiral staircase. Either they didn't expect to have to defend the light from attackers or the designer was left handed. It is also possible the designer didn't even give it any thought and just let Pedro and his mate Sanchez build it as they liked.

The view from the top, when we got there after a few reversals caused by meeting large Spanish ladies on the stairs was worth the climb. It had stopped raining and the air had cleared and we could see a long way in all directions. We could even see more bits of modern sculpture in the grounds around the lighthouse which allowed us to identify a route which avoided them on our way out.

Returning to the aquarium car park, we decided that staying the night here was really not a very attractive prospect so we decamped to Puerto de San Pedro, which is a tiny little fishing port to the west and only a few kilometres from the lighthouse. This has a couple of large and decidedly sloping car parks but the lower one was a little more level than the one higher up so we pulled in here and having the place to ourselves we went for a gentle explore. There was a bar but it looked shut, a few boats drawn up and not much else so our walk didn't take very long to complete.

Around the edge of the car park wild geraniums grew and Mary collected a few cuttings which she put in a pot of water by the sink. If they survive the journey they would take their place at home beside the spider plant cuttings stolen from a window box outside a bar in Portugal which she filched the previous year.

Our view over the car park was westward and out to sea which promised a good sunset but after getting the camera out as the sky began to redden, a solid bank of cloud rolled in and my potentially award-winning sunset shot was lost. The sky looked particularly threatening and would have sent any shepherds in the area scurrying for shelter.

Our motorhome has a separate toilet with a washbasin and it can also double as a shower, as the mixer tap from the basin can turn itself into a spray head which clips onto the wall just above head height. We have grown to love this little luxury although when we first got the motorhome we were very reluctant to use the shower as we were worried about getting everything wet and how long it would take to dry out afterwards. As a result, we used campsites but eventually the attraction of aires proved too much and once we had used the on-board shower we wondered why we had ever been so scared of using it.

The next morning, while I was having a shower I heard Mary call out "the aires man is here" which left me a little puzzled and wondering if someone from the local municipality was here to try and collect some money from us. I need not have worried because it was the couple from the guidebook again, making a flying visit to take some snaps of the aire and its service point; "could be cleaner" I can almost see written in the next edition. With a wave they were gone before I could finish dressing but with something like a few hundred aires to revisit I guess they don't have time to chin wag.

To the End of the Earth - Cabo Fisterre

Although we were staying at a little port on the western outskirts of A Coruña we had to drive back towards the city in order to escape further westwards. On the map we could see there was a toll road leading in the right direction but we were in no hurry and if possible we wanted to avoid handing over more money than necessary in order to travel around Spain. The satnav can be set to "Avoid Tolls" but I was feeling too lazy to rummage around in its settings to select this option but from the map it looked as though if we set the town of Arteixo as a via point we would take a non-toll road in the direction we wanted to go.

This worked but we did need to do some dead reckoning at one point as there has been a lot of road building around A Coruña and there were stretches where the satnav maps, which were supposed to be the latest edition, didn't recognise anything remotely looking like a road. We had had the same problem entering the previous day and it is a slightly weird sensation looking at the GPS screen and notice you appear to be driving through a green field, a fact which is contradicted by the view out of the windscreen.

Our diversion to the walls of Lugo had meant we had already missed some of the north coast of Galicia so places such as Viveiro and the exciting sounding *Punta de la Estaca de Bares*, the northernmost point of the Galician coast will have to wait for another trip. I have a friend who takes weeks to do what we had done in just a few days but his Spanish tours can last the best part of six months and we simply didn't have that sort of time. Why we don't have that much time is a slightly vexed question. We are both retired and should be able to take as long as we want off but family commitments and a niggling but I hope unfounded suspicion we might get bored if we were away too long has meant while each trip in the motorhome has been longer than the previous we are still some distance short of taking off for six months at a time. There is certainly a trick to it, a sort of Slow Food Movement for travelling and having the courage, there is no other word for it, to drive perhaps only a few miles each day and then pull over and enjoy a new view.

But as already admitted we have not reached such a Zen like state so it was in lightning tour mode we headed first for Malpica de

Bergantiños which is a very busy little fishing port near the first major headland west of A Coruña.

The road is a dead end but we turned round in the harbour although for anyone in a larger motorhome I would advise staying out of the town as the road we took was fairly steep down to the harbour and the room at the bottom limited for turning.

The harbour at Malpica de Bergantiños

We then followed the coast road off which many roads go to the headlands and more villages and ports. It would take days to see them all and some day we must, but we stayed on the through road before stopping at Muxia for lunch.

This was a much more motorhome friendly place with a couple already here in the car park and with other level areas nearby which I am sure you could overnight on.

Muxia

Stone granary or *horreo*

We also saw on this bit of coast one of the stone crosses by the road which mark shipwrecks along this coast and which give it its name, the *Costa da Morte* but as is often the case there was nowhere to pull over and stop to photograph the cross. The *Costa da Morte*, meaning of course the Coast of Death, stretches west from Muxia and has been the scene of many shipwrecks and much loss of life.

A particular feature of this area are the stone built granaries or *horreos* which are used to store grain and maize away from the damp and pests. These are seen elsewhere in Spain but I think the ones in Galicia are unique in being made of stone though we did see a few made from decidedly untraditional concrete.

The one on the previous page is quite small, there are a few over 30m long and many also have crosses on the roof. The practice dates back to Roman times and these granaries are everywhere partly perhaps because Galician farms are generally small as a result of estates being divided up amongst the children following the death of the parents I believe. The western end of the *Costa da Morte* is at Cabo Fisterre or Finisterre, thought for a long time to be the most westerly point of Europe but now more frequently known as the most westerly point of mainland Spain.

The laurels for the most westerly point of Europe are held by the Cabo da Roca in Portugal which is reputedly a bit touristy like Land's End and to be avoided unless you can go early or out of season or even more like Land's End, best avoided entirely.

The lighthouse or *faro* is housed in a fairly low building but perched on the granite of the cape high above the sea.

The lighthouse at Cabo Fisterre

This point on the coast is where pilgrims on the Camino traditionally come to burn their dirty clothes before entering Santiago de Compostela and we found a group doing just that, ceremonially burning some socks at one of the several burning spots below the lighthouse. The smell of burning socks was not something we had expected to greet us at such a romantic and dramatic spot.

About five hundred metres north west of the lighthouse, down a gravel track, is the little parking area used by motorhomes. You might just be able to see our vehicle on the right of this picture taken from near the lighthouse.

The aire at Cabo Fisterre

It would be nice to think we were going to spend the night at the most westerly point of Spain, and everything I had read suggested we were more or less there but we were not. The most westerly point of mainland Spain is Cabo Touriñán which was about ten kilometres further north from where we were. It is of course largely academic in that it only juts a *tiny* bit further west but clearly we have to go back there and try again. There is a lighthouse at Cabo Touriñán which from Google maps looks as if it might just have room for overnight parking so another trip to Galicia needs to be arranged. If only to see the flowers again.

***Drimia maritima*, or sea squill**

We were parked looking west with nothing between us and North America except a lot of sea. The position must see some spectacular sunsets and we had high hopes, unfortunately after a promising start the clouds were again just not right but we enjoyed the view anyway, which we shared with a stone giant, the head of which you should be able to see on the right hand side of the photograph below.

A notable feature of the landscape south from Cabo Fisterre are the Rias Baixas which can be seen as a series of four deep indentations in the coast stretching from Cabo Fisterre down to Vigo. This was the coastline we were to explore over the next few days. We also discovered after we had left the region they make some very good wine here with over twenty thousand vineyards involved in production. All I can say is the vineyards must be well hidden because

I don't remember seeing a single one although the Rias Baixas wine I tried much later elsewhere in Spain was memorable.

The giant looks west from the aire

The West Coast of Galicia – The Rias Baixas

We left Cabo Fisterre after a night during which we were woken by a couple of very heavy showers but fortunately we weren't washed off the cliff and the gravel track was firm enough for us to get back onto the tarmac road. Despite the complete lack of facilities I can't recommend this spot enough but I think later in the year (we were there in mid-June) you would want to arrive by midday to have a chance of getting in but it is a dramatic place to stay a night even if it isn't *quite* the most westerly point of Spain.

After shopping at the nearby town of Cee for provisions to keep us going for the next three days or so we followed the coast road slowly for the rest of the morning.

It really was a stunning landscape at this time of the year with the gorse and broom in full blossom.

Broom grew along the sides of the road

The broom generally grew lower down, beside the road but the hillsides above the road were covered in a great yellow carpet of gorse.

Gorse covered the hills

Our route took us through some interesting towns, particularly Muros which has very narrow little streets behind the waterfront and we ended the day at the aire at Praia de Mañóns. The service point for which was on the approach road a couple of hundred metres from the aire, which itself was just a mixed car park really.

The beach here is very sheltered, but it isn't really a swimming beach even if the water had been warmer. It was extremely shallow and the margins of the beach had a lot of slimy green seaweed and also masses of what looked like cling film. It was soft to touch and broke apart if you poked it with your boot. I have no idea what it was but it didn't look pleasant. The stuff can be easily seen along the tideline and nearest the camera in the photograph below. The next day we moved a little further down the coast, stopping on the way for a walk on the Illa de Arousa which is a little island joined to the mainland by a long low bridge. The southern half of the island is a nature reserve, which we struggled at first to find. You would think the phrase "southern half of the island" would describe somewhere hard to miss but somehow we managed it. The trick was to follow the signs to the campsite as the signs to the reserve had obviously been stolen or spirited away for some nefarious reason.

The beach at Praia de Mañóns

After eventually finding the reserve we parked up and had an early lunch, then set out on the short circular walk round the reserve. Unfortunately, our walk got off to a shaky start because two men were cutting the path with strimmers and they made it very clear the path was closed until they had finished.

The west side of Illa de Arousa

However, any circular walk has two options, clockwise or anticlockwise so we chose the former instead and hoped the men would have completed their work by the time we returned to the start.

The sea was very shallow here as well and full of rocks of all sizes sticking up out of the water. It reminded me somewhat of the Channel Islands, but without the huge tides. We had a delightful walk, glimpsing a party of linnets and eventually seeing the green woodpecker which we had heard calling almost since we arrived and we didn't have to reverse our steps due to obstructive brush cutters, the path clearing had been completed by the time we finished. It was also by then the middle of the afternoon so they had probably gone to lunch.

Our intention was to stop at a campsite at Sanxenxo for the night but we found it closed but close by was a commercial aire which turned out to be a real gem. It had terraced grass pitches, electricity, a free washing machine and was positioned just above a beach. The beach itself was most curious because it had sand which sang or squeaked as you walk over it. This is a phenomenon I've only come across once before – on a beach in Kentra Bay in Western Scotland, though singing sands as they are called are known from a number of locations around the world. The effect seems to happen when the grains are all of a very similar size.

Because it was so pleasant here we decided to stay a couple of nights at Sanxenxo then afterwards start to move inland and eventually southwards for the sun. Although we had had some pleasant weather during our stay in Galicia the outlook for the west coast was not great so the Grand Plan of dropping down through Portugal was postponed and added to the growing list headed "We Must Do This Some Other Time". We really should come back to Galicia if only because we somehow missed out on the seafood for which the area is famed, apart from the local mussels which I cooked while we stayed at Sanxenxo.

The bill for the aire came to eight Euros a night including electricity and the use of the free washing machine. What a great place, worth making a detour for as the Michelin guides say about the best restaurants.

We didn't immediately head inland but continued to follow the coast southwards, stopping for lunch just past Vigo at the Cabo Silleiro where there are old gun emplacements dotted on the cliffs near the lighthouse. Some still had old gun barrels sticking out from them. The bunkers were built in the 1940s to protect the port of Vigo but were abandoned some decades years ago. I have found out subsequently they are worth visiting but our main target today was the Celtic ruins, Castro de Santa Trega. These are a couple of kilometres from and almost vertically above A Guarda, which is at the very bottom left hand corner of Galicia on the north bank of the mouth of the Miño river as the Spaniards call it. On the opposite bank the Portuguese know this river, and the region, as the Minho.

Castro de Santa Trega was discovered in 1913 when a path was being cut. What they found, subsequent research showed was a Celtic settlement which was built up during the Iron Age, reaching its peak in the period of the second and first centuries BC.

The settlement was enclosed by a wall and filled with round stone houses with thatched roofs. The population is estimated to have been between three and six thousand and the site has still only been partially excavated but you can see more than enough to gain an impression of what it would have been like to have lived there.

Round houses at Castro de Santa Trega

On a sunny day we could have seen it all but unfortunately this wasn't a sunny day and the summit was wreathed in low cloud and rain. Through the gloom we could see numerous remains of the little houses. At first glance they look to be positioned at random but research has shown they are in small family groups of about half a dozen huts set around common courtyards, extended families probably with several generations living together. The picture below, taken in the gloom of low cloud shows a reconstructed house and around it are the circular remains of the original houses.

The road up to the site and the little museum at the top of the hill is steep and very twisty but at least the low cloud meant we couldn't see the drop. The museum is worth visiting if for no other reason than having driven all the way to the top it would be silly not to visit it, but all the captions on the exhibits are in Spanish so some of the history of the place was lost on us.

We ended the day at another commercial aire in a forest at Outomuro. This had electricity, a proper service point plus toilets and showers. Payment was on an honesty system; you filled in a form with your details, enclosed a ten Euro note and popped it in the little post box. We were the only customers but no doubt it would be busier later in the year.

Portugal (Briefly)

The next day we headed for Bragança in Portugal, driving through on and off heavy rain until we turned off south on the ZA925 near Puebla de Sanabria at which point the rain stopped and the sun tried to appear. We then travelled into the Parque Natural de Montesinho in Portugal on an interesting road designed by someone who didn't own a ruler or straight edge. Bend left, bend right, bend left, *ad infinitum*. The road had more bends in it than in one of Uri Gellar's spoons.

The hillsides had the flowering gorse, seen earlier, but also a white broom, *Retama raetam* which flowers a little earlier than the yellow species and was beginning to go over.

White broom, *Retama raetam*

The aire at Bragança was pretty full when we arrived, but we found one of last few remaining spots and I felt any late arrivals were probably going to have a squeeze. I needn't have worried as it turned out, because there was lots of room for more motorhomes, I just lacked the experience and imagination to realise where they could be put. After lunch we wandered up to the Citadel above the aire.

Bragança Citadel

This being the First of May and a holiday the tower was closed but we had a pleasant walk around the top of the wall. Unlike at Lugo you can't go all the way round and annoyingly having come to a dead end you find there is no way down and you have to retrace some of your steps.

On some of the older buildings we came across a variety of masons' marks on the stones. The purpose of these marks is not really known. They may be linked to payment, sometimes they show the alignment required of the stone and some may be quarry marks. The problem seems to be though aspects of building these great historic structures may be well documented in old records showing who paid for them and the cost and timescale there are no real descriptions of how the actual craftsmen worked. We might for example, know what they were paid or how many holidays they were allowed, but how they actually worked does not seem to have been seen to have been of sufficient importance for anyone to write it down. A bit like painting I suppose, there are galleries of portraits of the famous all around the world but it takes a Lowry to record the working people.

The walls around the citadel, Bragança

Mysterious masons' marks

Return to Spain

The following morning we found ourselves surrounded by vehicles that had arrived during the previous evening and night and which were now parked in every available crevice. I am sure the population must have doubled from the point where I thought the place was full.

But now it was time to begin the retreat from Portugal as our presence here was more of a geographical accident. Cutting through the north western corner of Portugal was the best way to go to southern Spain from Galicia. Shortly after leaving Portugal, on the road to Zamora, we entered an area where the field boundaries were made with flat stones. I had seen a few of these in Galicia but there use here was quite extensive.

The photograph below shows branches being used to close the gaps, elsewhere we saw drystone walling serving the same gap filling role.

Field boundaries made with flat stones

There are a few of these "clapper" fences in Devon so it isn't a unique method of construction, but I suspect it is very old.

Our intentions today were to stop in Zamora, have a look around then move to Salamanca for a couple of nights. There were two aires I knew of, both without any facilities and we parked up for our visit in the one on the west side, which was very close to the city walls.

This seems a good overnight halt if you don't need facilities although there is a drinking fountain in the children's playground next door but I think you would struggle to fill up more than small drinking water bottles from it. Zamora still has quite a lot of the old walls remaining, which are built on a rock escarpment in places. We entered the city through a gate close to the castillo and cathedral, where we found a wedding being held so we stayed outside out of politeness. Though I am not sure if anyone would have noticed if we had gone in as plenty of others were who didn't look like they were part of the wedding party. Typical British reserve on our part I suppose, the locals seemed unconcerned by the wedding and either ignored it or had a good stare.

The cathedral itself has an interesting dome with fish scale tiling and a nearby church had some nesting storks.

Roof of Zamora cathedral

Nesting storks

The old city also has a castillo which is separated from the rest of the walled town by a moat cut into the rock, which was more or less the only interesting feature of the structure. Inside there wasn't a lot to see if I am brutally honest, it had been beautifully restored but was such a hotchpotch of styles, modifications and eras it was hard for the ignorant tourist like me to make sense of it all.

What I could make better sense of were the sculptures of naked ladies. This one is a dancer I think.

Dancer?

We also saw more of those cryptic masons' marks. Is there some mystery like the Da Vinci Code to unravel here?

Salamanca

Though Zamora was interesting it didn't really have much of a wow factor for us, though that is probably down to our ignorance and lack of appreciation for what we were seeing. Zamora has more Romanesque churches than any other city in Europe but perhaps because the weather was overcast and we still hadn't settled down into "holiday mode" or because we just visited too quickly it somehow failed to impress, though the storks were nice to see. Our next destination, Salamanca, home to some of the finest Renaissance and Plateresque architecture in Spain, as opposed to just having lots of churches, looked much more promising.

Salamanca has a long history having been home to Celtic tribes, besieged by Hannibal and then adopted by the Romans as an important commercial hub for their Hispanic empire. Conquered by the Arabs from north Africa in AD712 the city found itself on the front line between the Christian kings of the north and the Arabs in the south. An important event in 1218 was the establishment of a university here and today Salamanca remains one of the most important university cities in Spain.

There was a choice of places we could have stayed which ranged from a couple of basic aires without facilities close to the city to several campsites on the outskirts. We chose Camping Don Quijote at Cabrerizos on the western side of Salamanca primarily because it was beside the Rio Tormes alongside which runs a footpath into the city. This was a well-run site and surprisingly busy, which came as a small shock after our fairly lonely existence up until this point.

The following morning we walked the six kilometres into Salamanca along the riverside path. This varied from a wide gravel track at the start, fully paved near the city and with a narrow path close to the river bank in the middle.

It took us just over an hour and a half of level walking, which I did in walking sandals though boots would have been needed if the weather had been damp. The last part of the walk is amongst buildings, including shops and businesses and it was all quite busy, there was an open air market going on at one place but by following our noses in a few places where we had to move away from the river we reached our first landmark. This was the Puente Romano, twenty six arches, fifteen of which are original from its First Century AD construction.

Puente Romano, Salamanca

The building behind the bridge in the photograph above is the cathedral which we visited next, not because we had any sort of itinerary planned, more a case of it being big and hard to miss.

Unlike the cathedral at Zamora there was no wedding taking place so we decided to look inside. After a sharp intake of breath when we spotted the five Euro entrance fee we nevertheless paid up and I am glad we did. We were each given a device like a large mobile phone into which you typed the number shown on boards around the building. So, starting at number one you hear an introduction to the cathedral, in English, and then proceed to station number two and so on.

Although not obvious from the outside there are two cathedrals, the old and the new and your self-guided tour starts in the old. I took a lot of photographs in the Cathedral with the asa setting cranked up to maximum but the pictures came out a bit too grainy and I really should have used a tripod as only a few pictures were really good enough to keep.

However, there was a great deal to see in the Cathedral(s) and I strongly recommend you take the tour and a tripod, to sneak in another zeugma.

When we came out of the Cathedral we found it had started raining.

After lunch, three courses, wine and coffee for twelve Euros which seemed very reasonable for a touristy place, we attempted to walk off some of the ingested calories seeing other parts of the old city.

The Convento de San Estaban was another impressive building with a cheery image of the stoning of St Stephen above the entrance.

Convento de San Estaban, Salamanca

The facade is considered a fine example of Plateresque art, very finely carved with impressive detail of the brutality. (next page)

Stoning of St Stephen, Convento de San Estaban

The final photograph in this section is of the Fifteenth Century Torre del Clavero which after seeing we took a ten Euro taxi ride back to the campsite, having done enough walking for the day. There were other places in Salamanca to visit but they were closed in the afternoon. The Convento de las Dueñas, with its carvings of demons, skulls and tormented faces will have to wait (yes, you've guessed it) for another trip.

Torre del Clavero, Salamanca

Ávila

Spain is full of surprises, we left Salamanca to visit Ávila to see the famous walls there but it turned out we were more impressed by the cathedral. Ávila has of course walls, it is renowned for its walls and if you hadn't heard of them they have a little notice telling you what you need to know.

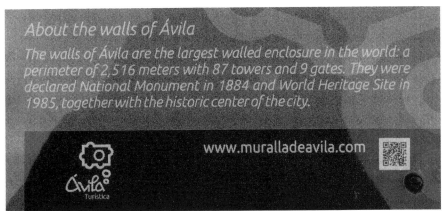

All you need to know about the walls of Ávila

And the walls themselves are fairy tale stuff.

The walls of Ávila

We entered through one of the gates and headed towards the other end of the city, passing a plaza which was unique so far on the trip as it was dry because it wasn't raining. The cathedral, which we were heading for is unfinished as there should be a second tower on the right of the entrance, but a banking crisis or something similar brought construction to a halt. And we think recessions are a new thing.

The women sitting outside was really nice, it only cost us one Euro to leave after our visit.

Entrance to Ávila cathedral

Note the two scaly figures above the door. These give a hint of some of the weird things to be found inside.

The Cathedral is a classic Gothic structure, all soaring heights and designed to put you in your place in the pecking order of cosmic and temporal order.

One carving we came across depicted a monkey (I think) grabbing the hair of very hairy lady.

The audio commentary (another follow the numbers game) did not elaborate on what this was supposed to depict. It was probably either too rude or they didn't know.

Hairy lady chased by hairy monkey, Ávila cathedral

The Slaughter of the Innocents, Ávila Cathedral

115

But some of the carvings were easier to admire. Here (previous page) the Slaughter of the Innocents when Herod ordered the death of all young children after the birth of Jesus.

There were several works similar to this, all carved in the Sixteenth Century and with very fine detail.

Vaulted roof, Ávila cathedral

The heart of the cathedral dates from around the thirteen hundreds and one of the walls at this point doubles up on the outside as part of the City wall. This area is made from an extraordinary red and white stone.

There were plenty of other carvings showing the usual weirdness, here bedtime stories for cattle.

Curious biblical scene, Ávila cathedral

And of course those sinister masons had been here. Don't tell anyone but one of these stones (next page) may be upside-down.

Ávila was a surprise, famed for its walls but within them was a stunning secret. My eyes had been significantly opened on what Spain had to offer and all for the price of a Euro to the lady on the door.

Masons' marks again

Over the Sierra de Gredos

One factor of Spain constantly surprises me and it's one I've already mentioned; just how mountainous it is. Arriving as we did in Santander you can see mountains in almost every direction looking landward. The Pyrenees of course are very well known, sitting along the border between France and Spain. Perhaps less well known, the Sierra Nevada way down in the south of Spain while perhaps lacking the impact of the Pyrenees does have the highest peak in mainland Spain, the 3,478 metre high Mulhacén. But as the view from Santander hints, you are never far from a mountain in Spain and leaving Ávila and driving south we had to cross over the Sierra de Gredos. This is a long range of mountains which starts west of Madrid then arcs around the north of the capital. It is not unknown in winter for the main roads crossing the range to be blocked with snow, which can be an unexpected hazard to the traveller heading for the sunshine of the south.

Our route, on the N502 from Ávila, took us initially south west then we turned south. It was soon clear to us this was a very popular road with motorcyclists and we saw several groups of them, enjoying the bends and a good road surface.

There were a couple of cols to go over, the Puente de Menga (1,654m) and the slightly lower but decidedly more breezy Puerto del Pico where I stopped to take a photograph. A strong wind had built up during the afternoon and the 'van was being strongly buffeted. When I stepped out of the vehicle take the picture below I was convinced this was the strongest wind I had ever tried to stand up in. I had to set the camera to an exposure of one two thousandths of a second in an attempt to counter the shaking of the camera caused by the wind.

What I didn't recognize while I was struggling to take the picture of the impressive view southwards was right below me was a wide road looping away into the distance made from large slabs of stone. This was a genuine Roman road, built by them over two thousand years ago to link Merida and Ávila and to transport minerals extracted from the Sierra de Gredos. In post-Roman times it was used for transporting livestock but it has remained in remarkably good condition to the present day. None of which I knew anything about at the time and I only learned this later when I looked at the photograph and saw the road. If you search online for the *Calzada romana en Puerto del Pico* you will find a number of photographs taken from the very spot where I took mine. This is the photograph I took; a prominent bend in the Roman road is in the foreground. A modern road can be seen on the right of the picture and the Roman road can be seen running off to the left and into the distance.

View south from the Puerto del Pico, Sierra de Gredos, with Roman road in the foreground

Urban Aire

We stopped for the night at an aire in Talavera de la Reina which turned out to be probably the least atmospheric halts of the trip so far.

On reflection delete "probably". This wasn't an aire in the countryside, it was simply some parking bays marked for motorhomes in a city street. It was also a fairly busy road and was in one of those dingy parts of a city of the sort you often see when entering a city by a train. But it was free and convenient, which were enough plus points to make it our halt for the night.

The traffic continued in the road until very late but eventually it did stop. There was a brief moment of excitement in the early evening when with much sounding of sirens several fire engines left from a gateway about one hundred yards away. What joy, I thought; it seemed we were parked next to a fire station. However, a few minutes later they all came quietly back again so I guessed it had only been a drill. But it was nice to know we will be well looked after if we have a fire and perhaps we should break out the deep fat fryer, have some chips followed by a pudding set alight with brandy. Of course should a massive conflagration in Talavera de la Reina start like the Great Fire of London in the Spanish equivalent of a bakery in Pudding Lane, the *Panadería* in the *Carril del Postre* at three o'clock in the morning you can be sure the *Bomberos* would not be so cruel as to let us sleep through it and would make sure we would be well awake to witness their actions.

I took this photograph (next page) of us the following morning. In the building on the left was a machine which went "squeak - aargh" about every fifteen seconds, but in a civilised fashion it didn't start until after breakfast. You can also see a light from a stadium in the background and I suspect this aire could be *very* noisy when there is a football match on.

The "aire" at Talavera de la Reina. Note the motorhome symbol on the road

Toledo

We only had a fairly short eighty kilometre drive to Toledo from Ávila so we took the minor CM 4000 road, avoiding the dual carriageway. We drove past vines and a lot of olive trees of which Spain has legion of course. The fields were very green and a great contrast they will look at the end of the summer when everything will be scorched brown.

There were a lot of poppies too though these are not a new phenomenon in Spain. Laurie Lee described walking in fierce heat beside poppies in the 1930s in his book "As I Walked Out One Midsummer Morning".

> …*walking a white dust road straight as a canal banked by shimmering wheat and poppies.*"

Roadside poppies

Although there are a couple of car parks close to Toledo which can be used we headed for the El Greco campsite which we found with little difficulty, thanks to the wonders of GPS. Our plan was to stay here for a couple of nights and explore the city, which has a long history and many striking buildings.

After passing through the imposing entrance gates of the campsite we were amazed to find ourselves in a tree-lined avenue. This was a bit of a step up from the usual car park aire or roadside space with machines which go "squeak – aargh" beside them.

From the campsite reception office we had a good view of the city.

Distant view of Toledo

After lunch we walked the easy three kilometres into the city, entering by the medieval Puente de San Martin.

Puente de San Martin, Toledo

Our plan was to explore the city properly the next day but we couldn't resist a quick walk around. After crossing the Puente de San Martin we headed uphill, passing first the monastery of San Juan de los Reyos which is curiously decorated on the outside with the chains of Christian prisoners liberated on the re-taking of Granada. Looking at the map and the available time we had we decided a quick visit to the Synagogue of St Maria la Blanca (next page) would make a gentle introduction to Toledo. The synagogue is a former mosque, which was very evident on the inside as this not very good photograph shows. The next morning we entered Toledo using the escalators on the west side of the city, having tried the more traditional route of penitents the previous day and ascended countless steps in the process. A city with escalators? Yes, it really does have escalators and they are a very clever idea as inconveniently for tourists the city fathers built Toledo on the top of a hill and all the modern approach roads and car parks are much lower down. This means to visit Toledo you have to gain altitude and the escalators take you effortlessly up to the level of the old city. We managed to squeeze into a gap between the crowds which were flowing into the city from the numerous coaches arriving all the time.

Synagogue of St Maria la Blanca. Toledo

The escalators of Toledo

We headed directly for the cathedral, which is one of the main draws of Toledo and clearly this fact is well known because everyone else we had shared the escalators with seemed to be going in the same direction.

It cost us ten Euros each to get in, for which price I hoped the custodians of the cathedral had been up late the previous night polishing and scrubbing and generally making it presentable for us. A somewhat uncharitable thought, because they could double or treble the entrance price and it would still be worth it. As we were to find out.

The cathedral is the classic Gothic model, all slender pillars and high roof so at first glance not massively different to the two previous cathedrals we had visited.

But the details here are in a different league and you are going to have to live with my grainy photographs because Toledo cathedral was simply stunning.

They have some quite big paintings too, note the figure in the bottom left for scale.

Tall painting, Toledo cathedral

This is the Transparente so called because it is pierced in several places to allow light into the room beyond. It is massive. The round black thing hanging from the roof with tassels dangling from it in the upper right is a cardinal's hat. Don't think these folk have no sense of fun.

The Transparente, Toledo cathedral

This feature was just breath-taking. It is a window or more accurately a skylight, a bit like a periscope high above your head which is placed to give light to the Transparente. In the skylight are figures, some of them looking down at you. Look in the bottom right of the picture for the best ones. This is three dimensional carving and sculpture, not *trompe l'oeil*

Airy skylight with figures looking down

They have a few normal sized paintings too from the likes of Velázquez, Goya and most famously locally, El Greco.

El Greco is synonymous with Toledo, born in Crete (hence the name "the Greek") he trained in Venice and Rome before coming to Toledo in 1577 where he stayed until his death in 1614. The city does make a big thing of this and who can blame them. There is a museum dedicated to El Greco and no doubt El Greco 'fridge magnets are available from appropriate outlets.

The carving behind the high altar is extraordinary. It was completed around 1500.

The High Alter, Toledo cathedral

The owl and the monkeys, Toledo cathedral

The choir had some interesting seats to use with misericords where you rested your bottom when you were supposed to be standing. The word comes from the Latin *misericordia* meaning "mercy". These misericords had some seriously weird carving. The example on the previous page appears to be two monkeys spoon feeding an owl. What is that all about? In addition to the misericords the backs of the chairs each had a different carving showing the retaking of cities from the Moors.

At this point, somewhat sore of foot, we sought lunch and decided to splash out on a twenty two Euro menu in a little restaurant which had walls covered in things associated with hunting, plus various stuffed birds and animals. After lunch we went to visit the Alcázar, the scene of a siege during the Civil War when it was held by some of Franco's folk against the townspeople. Several hundred women and children were also caught up in the siege plus a hundred or so left wing prisoners, who were never heard of again. During the siege the attackers captured the sixteen year old son of the commander, Colonel Moscardó, who they telephoned and told him they would shoot his son if he did not surrender. It is recorded Moscardó told his son to "die like a patriot" echoing the words of Guzman during the siege of Tarifa in 1294. Things subsequently got so desperate in the Alcázar the defenders resorted to eating their horses. Franco eventually sent a large force to relieve the siege and after taking Toledo much blood was shed in reprisals. It is now a military museum and is shut on Wednesday.

The day of our visit was of course a Wednesday.

In compensation for the closed Alcázar we found an interesting building nearby which was covered in bullet holes. It should probably be some sort of monument to the Civil War now but of course the collective amnesia which Spain exhibits about this period ensures it stays in the background and from the signs saying it was for sale I suspect it will soon be demolished.

So we wandered a little further on to the eastern edge of the town where we dropped down and followed the riverside path. My wife pointed out a heron on the far bank, a not particularly unusual sighting, and then she said "there's another bird over there". This bird was much more interesting and the first I have ever seen, it was a Night Heron. The photograph below shows the bird sitting in a fig. The white flash you can see projecting back from its head is a long plume formed from two or three feathers. Both the males and females have this characteristic. Unlike the head plumes of the little egret these don't seem to have been discovered by 19th Century hat makers otherwise the bird would probably now be extinct.

Bullet scarred building, Toledo

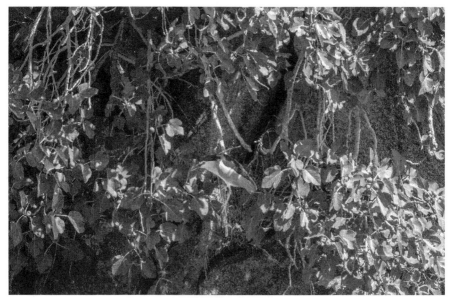

Night heron

Night Herons, as we discovered are seen in daylight, partly because no one has told them their name but also because it probably had young to feed.

Stone re-cycling, Toledo

And just when you think Toledo can't get any better, you see a stone built into a bridge upside down. Possibly put in place by the two masons who built the staircase going the wrong way in the Tower of Hercules at A Coruña.

We eventually left the city on the down escalator with what looked like a group of South Koreans, fortunately avoiding any injuries from their selfie-sticks which were being brandished with enthusiasm.

Our convoluted route to Toledo is shown below.

Warning Lights

The following day was a bit mixed. We started off with a gentle drive south from Toledo on the CM 403 through the Montes de Toledo. Part of these hills are a nature reserve, the Parque Natural de Cabañeros where the shepherds use a distinctive conical shelter, like a thatched witch's hat called a *chozo* but we couldn't see any from the route we took but admittedly we were outside the reserve itself. Successful *chozo* spotting would require a dedicated journey I think.

Lavender was common along the roadside. It is what I know as French Lavender though it is also called Spanish Lavender, which is probably a more appropriate name as we *were* in Spain.

As lunch time approached a warning suddenly lit up on the dashboard, "consult handbook" it said. So we stopped for lunch at a conveniently placed reservoir and I consulted. As an aside, where we stopped was a reasonable wild camping spot. If you approach the Embalse de Torre de Abraham from the north, just as the road bends left take the old road, which goes straight on. Don't go too far as the road literally goes into the lake, so stop short before things get too wet.

But if not looking for a wild camping spot this is a remote place to break down.

Consultations with the handbook suggested high transmission oil temperature, which was unexpected as we were going down a gentle hill when it came on. After knocking off the remains of last night's chorizo and chickpea stew, accompanied by a Lidl's bake-it-yourself mini-baguette, things looked better when I fired up to a dashboard free of reading recommendations.

Uncertain what the problem was I decided to stick to main roads for the day and so we missed the Tablas de Daimiel wetlands and went straight for a campsite in the Lagunas de Ruidera. This is a green and fertile place in an otherwise arid region. It is a series of lakes each one just a little above the next, each feeding the one below by waterfalls and subterranean rivers.

The system of underground water in this area is being used to support an expansion of vineyards, of which we saw many newly planted during our drive. Unfortunately, this is having an inevitable impact above ground. The Lagunas themselves seem safe as they are above the point of extraction but the Tablas de Daimiel, which are an important wildlife refuge are suffering from a drop in water level.

Lagunas de Ruidera

Fortunately the camp bar was suffering no such drought and that evening we enjoyed a cold beer and then sat out quite late, enjoying the warmth in the air an unbitten by insects. Cathedrals are fine but you can't beat a good warm evening and a cold drink.

On our journey that day we had also bought a little mint plant. It didn't look like the classic mint of English mint sauce variety, but exactly what sort of mint it was we were uncertain at the time. However, we now had the three volatile ingredients: mint, sherry and a sort of Sprite to make up some Rebujito. A drink we had heard about from a friend living in Spain who said the drink was a favourite at the September "*Feria del Día*" (local festival) in the town where he lived. We just needed to find a suitable opportunity to try it.

Ingredients for Rebujito:

Manzanilla, Seven-up or Sprite, Ice, Leaves of *hierbabuena* (a type of mint)

Method:

One part Manzanilla to two parts Seven-up, add lots of ice and the mint leaves to a jug.

The identity of *hierbabuena* was a topic of much discussion but at least we now had a mint of some sort.

Into the Forest

After leaving the Lagunas de Ruidera (another place we could/should have stayed longer) we headed for Cazorla, which is the main gateway into the Parque Natural Sierras de Cazorla. This is an area of gorges and forests and the source of the river Guadalquivir which flows from here through Seville and then into the sea at Sanlúcar de Barrameda, which is in its own way a source of another fine liquid, Manzanilla sherry.

It was a steep climb up from Cazorla until we reached the top of the first ridge, the park seems to consist of several ridges running north east to south west like a rumpled blanket.

The view looking down into the valley of the Guadalquivir

We dropped down from where the previous photograph was taken into the valley then took what soon became a gravel track into the forest. After about thirty kilometres of fairly easy driving we pulled over into a tiny car parking area beside the track. We had been following the GPS coordinates for a campsite listed on a website but it was nowhere to be found. This may have been because, as we subsequently discovered, the coordinates listed were wrong. It wasn't by any means a disaster as we had food and water for an overnight stay in the forest and so that was exactly what we decided to do.

Forest camping, Cazorla

It was a pretty remote spot and there were extensive signs of wild boar foraging just yards from where we were parked. The diggings were remarkably large and extensive as if a mechanical excavator had gone berserk.

We had a very quiet night in the forest apart from a car pulling up at about nine o'clock when a young man jumped out and excitedly or perhaps drunkenly asked the way to Cazorla. I point back down the way he had come to which he responded by jumping back into the car with his wife/girlfriend and speeding off in the exact opposite direction to which I had pointed. We didn't see or hear from him again.

The next day, not really sure where *we* were going either we continued north easterly on the track, passing through Nava de Pablo.

There was a tricky section just before we left the trees with a steep unguarded drop, edge washed away by rain, recent rock fall on the track, that sort of thing, but fortunately we met no one coming the other way. This was a single track road with only occasionally encountered narrow passing places and zero opportunities for turning round. But the views were impressive when I had time to take my eyes off the road ahead.

Cazorla forest

We breathed a sigh of relief when the gradient levelled and the country opened up.

It was a false dawn, things got much worse. We took the road through places named on the map, Caserio de Don Domingo and Loma Gerica, but all we could see was the occasional house or *refugio*. I also had the 1:25k IGN map on my walking/cycling GPS but the map was pretty out of date I think and wasn't a lot of help. We simply decided to stay on the most used looking bit of track whenever there was a junction and head in a generally north easterly direction.

The worst stretch was when we followed a small valley down a gentle descent. The track jumped repeatedly from one side of the stream to the other, crossing the river bed each time. Fortunately there was very little water in the stream and it was only two or three inches deep but the crossings were rough and rocky. I kept having to get out on foot and survey each crossing, several times filling in the deepest ruts with extra stones.

We got through, a few crossing were really on the borderline and grates and crunches from underneath were evidence of this.

The plateau north east of Cazorla forest

The Cazorla forest is a great place to visit, enter from Cazorla but turn round at Nava de Pablo, don't go any further without a good cross-country vehicle under you. The track isn't difficult but it isn't built for motorhomes.

Heading for the Sea

Our plan after the forest was to cultivate our sun tans for a few days at Cabo de Gata, south east of Almeria and so we booked into the Los Escullos campsite which is on the east side of the cape.

To celebrate our eventful time in and escape from Cazorla we finally made up a jug of Rebujito. We may not have quite the right leaves, because we have we subsequently identified what we had was spearmint but it still made a fine refreshing drink for a Sunday lunchtime.

Rebujito

Instructions: transfer from jug to glass and then to mouth. Repeat until jug empty.

We had a lazy time at this site, doing a lot of reading but I did wander out one morning to take a few photographs.

The picture below shows the village of Los Escullos which is between the campsite and the coast. The square building is the Eighteenth Century Castillo de San Felipe. This region of the coast is very arid although there were the remains of old terracing but it must have been dry and desperate farming.

Los Escullos and the Castillo de San Felipe

European fan palm growing in arid scrub

The palm in the centre of the picture above is the European Fan Palm (*Chamaerops humilis*), the only palm native to Western Europe, the other European palm being the rare and protected Cretan Date palm (*Phoenix theophrasti*) which has a very limited distribution in the Eastern Mediterranean. The Cabo de Gata was to be our most southerly point on this trip. The experience of our previous visit to Spain is there wasn't a lot to be seen along the coast further west from here without going a very long way westward or heading inland to say the Alpujarras at the southern end of the Sierra Nevada.

The principal problems with the coast between where we were and interesting points further west are plastic and concrete. The plastic are greenhouses which stretch all along the coast for growing tomatoes and other crops. The main greenhouse area ends around Motril but they cover vast areas though the only saving grace is the coast itself along here, even without the greenhouses wouldn't be particularly attractive. Further west, starting at Malaga, are a succession of heavily populated towns and popular tourist attractions like Torremolinos which stretch more or less to Gibraltar, which isn't somewhere that attractive to us either, we are hard to please. However, I would be being unfair to condemn the whole of the Spanish coast along this stretch. There will be some delightful spots, especially inland in regions seldom trodden by the tourist but time was against us exploring any further in that direction so we started to head back.

A Gassing Issue

Just before we had arrived at the Cabo de Gata we had diverted to a garage to fill up the on-board gas tank. Normally this is a painless procedure, I have the Spanish adaptor and with the tank only about a quarter full I expected it to take on a serious fill of gas. It didn't. After much faffing around, involving help from the man from the garage, we could barely get fifty cents worth of gas into the tank or to be more precise we spent fifty cents on gas which escaped during the attempted filling process. Clearly there was a problem.

I subsequently called the manufacturer of the gas tank and was advised how to try a different filling procedure next time we tried to fill up in an attempt to blow open the valve which might be sticking. This method involved a stealth approach to the gas tank, tricking it into a feeling that it wasn't about to be filled, and then hitting it with the full pressure of the gas.

Fortunately, the level of gas in the tank wasn't critical, and we had enough gas for a few more weeks, but as we drove away from the Capo de Gata area we found another Repsol garage to try and fill the tank a second time. The recommended procedure this time was to connect the hose but *not* squeeze the trigger, then press the button on the pump itself and when the hose was pressurized, squeeze the trigger on the filler and hope the rush of gas would open the valve. We tried. It didn't.

So a little depressed both mentally and in gas pressure terms (a very weak zeugma) we followed the coast road north from Carboneras where a few kilometres beyond the town we stopped for lunch beside the sea. We pulled off the main road onto what looked like the remains of the old coast road and then onto a gravel parking area where a French registered motorhome was already parked.

This would make a nice place to overnight I thought. It had its own tiny little beach of clean sand amongst rocks though I only glimpsed this briefly as the little beach was already occupied, by a lady from the French motorhome I assumed, there being no other vehicles around. The problem was she was considerably under-dressed compared to me, as in not wearing anything at all so not wishing to be considered a Meerkat I tactfully withdrew.

Nearby to where we were parked there was a large unfinished hotel, sitting on its own on an otherwise totally undeveloped coast. This hotel in-waiting is quite famous in its own discredited way as it

144

remains unfinished because the builders' forgot to get planning permission for it. Which isn't a unique occurrence in Spain and the insignificant technicality of not having planning permission hasn't stopped structures being built before and one can only speculate why this one was halted. The word "Mafia" written in large graffiti on the side of it may or may not be a hint.

Unfinished and unloved hotel

We will certainly go back to the Cabo de Gata; we only saw a tiny bit and the Cabo itself, as a headland not at all. There are some *salinas* on the west side where there were probably flamingos and other interesting birds but we now headed for Águilas, south of Murcia on the Costa Cálida, one of the lesser known costas and to Camping Bellavista, where we had stayed the previous year.

Águilas, Murcia

After nearly four weeks away I found I was at last beginning to detect the first signs of relaxation with no sudden urges to drive off to somewhere different. A typical day now started with a couple of lengths of the campsite pool followed by an hour or two with my nose stuck into my first Montalbano book, which turned out to be as enjoyable as the TV series. Then it would be time for lunch, it was a demanding life.

When not a lot is happening meals become an important part of the day and we were trying to live healthily, in every respect apart from our alcohol consumption which no doubt exceeded the recommended dosage by several points, but we were on holiday, as if that was a viable excuse.

This is what a typical lunch time meal looked like:

Salad lunch - with red wine

Essentially just lettuce plus a salad made of tomatoes, cucumber, and courgette and in this case chickpeas which is sometimes replaced by feta cheese. The courgette had been a relatively new discovery.

Sometimes as in this case cut it is cut into little chunks though our favourite method of preparation was to simply make thin shavings from an already peeled courgette using the potato peeler. The trick was just to pare the fleshy part of the vegetable and leave the core with the seeds untouched. Ideally this needs to be made a little while in advance so it can be dribbled with olive oil and then left so the juices combine with the oil to give the salad a bit of lubrication. You can add salt at this stage which draws out more water from the courgette but we do try to cut down on salt and we still find the result very tasty, though no doubt the TV chefs would declare that it needed "more seasoning". Other ingredients like red peppers can be added if desired to ring the changes and ensure we didn't eat *exactly* the same meal every day.

The salad was usually eaten with a selection of slices of chorizo, ham and cheese – of which we prefer the generally softer *semi-curado* over the more mature *curado*. Add mayonnaise (garlic *and* the ordinary sort in my greedy case) and yet more olive oil, lots of black pepper and this makes a good lunch for hot weather and we had hardly eaten any potatoes or bread for several weeks.

We didn't spend *all* our time lazing in the campsite, one day we drove a full kilometre or so to Águilas which is not a particularly historic town although it is overlooked by a little Eighteenth Century fort but it has a nice waterfront and plenty of places to eat and drink. It also has one of the wildest fiestas in Spain in February should you find yourselves in the area at this time and seek a diversion.

We parked beside the port and marina and after a bit of searching around to find the way we walked up a great many steps to the fort, where there is a little museum although again all the captions and descriptions of the exhibits were in Spanish but the view from the top was impressive and worth the walk.

The Cuatro Calas are a well-known series of coves and beaches around Águilas which we visited in the afternoon. One of our guidebooks claimed these were something special but after our visit we were unconvinced, mainly because of the amount of rubbish left by humans on or around them. When I say "unconvinced" I really think I mean disappointed. We visited Playa Taray first, which is one of the westernmost coves. The picture below shows it at its best, what you can't see off to the left are the dead palms, rubbish and the remains of fires lit on the beach.

The view from the fort looking down on Águilas

Playa Taray

On the other side of the headland in the picture above is Cala Cerrada, here looking attractive and matching the guidebook description.

Cala Cerrada

But if I had swung the camera a little to the right it would have been a very different picture. They have built a café right above the beach and next to it they were either building another one or a private house. What should have been a pristine location was simply being commercialised into oblivion. There are also caves cut into the soft rock, probably used by fishermen in days gone as storerooms. In days present they are by turn toilets and litter bins.

I should probably stop reading guide books.

After a few days of this relaxation I realised I couldn't put off updating my longhand diary any longer. It was at least two weeks out of date and needed some determined application of bottom to seat and pen to paper. This diary is where I use numbered stickers in an atlas to cross-reference with the appropriate entry in the diary. The idea is to create a visual reference in the atlas of places we have visited and my description of those places. Obsessive I know but it will keep me happy reading them in my twilight years.

While writing up the diary I was joined one by one by three of the campsite cats, which lay down near me. They weren't doing any harm so they snoozed through the morning beside me while I sweated over a hot pen.

At the end of the morning I called time on the diary and made a jug of Rebujito, which with patient application we were developing a distinct taste for.

Meanwhile, the cats, which I now called the Three Amigos, continued their exciting morning sleeping around my feet. I can't say I

149

am a cat fan but you can't blame the animals for acting according to their nature which by the example of the Three Amigos was to snooze all day, waking occasionally to chase some wildlife. A bit like dogs, who sleep all day, waking occasionally to chase cats.

However, lunchtime was approaching and we knew from previous experience these cats could be a nuisance when food arrived. So I tried my Mark 1 Non-Lethal Cat Deterrent. This consisted simply of flicking water at them. It worked but the range I could project the water was limited and the Three Amigos soon worked out just how close they could come in safety.

During lunch which today included feta cheese, I worked on a theoretical design for a Mark 2 Non-Lethal Cat Deterrent. Range seemed to be the key so perhaps a water bottle with a hole in the lid might function as an improvised water pistol? The other essential of the design was the non-lethality. We have seen some sorry looking cats on our travels but the Three Amigos were in show bench condition and either had some sort of quasi-official status here or were just very good at mugging food and had a lot of friends.

The problem was resolved after I returned from doing the washing up. The Three Amigos had vanished and we had accidentally discovered the Mark 3 Non-Lethal Cat Deterrent. Take away all prospect of food.

The gas refilling problem was still a concern, soon we were going to run out of gas which meant no cooking but more importantly we would not be able to run the refrigerator on gas, which is what we do on aires or sites without electricity. There are essentially two different sorts of refrigerator fitted to motorhomes. By far the most common are the absorption type which can run off gas and electricity, the other sort are made like a typical domestic refrigerator and have a compressor inside them. These run off twelve volts only but they work well in high ambient temperatures and are generally much more reliable than absorption designs. However, the convenience of being able to run off gas makes absorption refrigerators very popular and this is the type we have in our motorhome. For cooking we could always go and buy a little camping stove but the loss of the refrigerator would be a nuisance. Of course a refrigerator is just a modern luxury but it is very easy to be seduced by these conveniences. I camped with my parents from a very early age and in those days they didn't even have such a thing as a cool box and when we made a trip to Yugoslavia in the early sixties my mother brought butter with us in tins as that was the only way to store it without access to anywhere cool.

The motorhome world is a bit of a club and there are places online where you can post messages and ask questions. I am a regular on one such forum (www.motorhomefun.co.uk) and through this I put out a plea for help or suggestions on the gas problem. As a result I was able to make contact with another motorhome owner who lived only a short distance away on the outskirts of Lorca. Richard cheerfully agreed to lend us a gas bottle with regulator and hose which I would use to connect to the external BBQ on the motorhome. This solution had occurred to me earlier and the tank manufacturer also suggested it as a safe option to keep us running when the gas tank ran out. The reason for borrowing rather than buying a gas bottle was that technically we couldn't buy a new bottle in Spain without having the right sort of gas safety certificate for the motorhome, which we didn't have. Although it is apparently possible to find a supplier who will take cash and ask no questions it was easier to borrow one, especially as the bottle's owner was returning to the UK later in the year and would be staying not far from us, giving me the opportunity to return his very kindly lent equipment.

This is the reason in subsequent pictures of our motorhome you may see a red and grey Cepsa bottle chained to the tow bar. When we moved the bottle was carried inside firmly tied to the passenger seat rails.

Heading North Again

Before we left Águilas we did a bit of shopping for supplies and made a trip to the bank for cash then we drove a short way north along the coast to a strikingly positioned place near the Cabo Cope, just short of Calabardina, where we stopped for lunch.

The Beach south of Cabo Cope (visible in the distance)

This beach is a recognised stopover for motorhomes and gets extremely busy in the winter but we almost had it to ourselves in the middle of May. We would certainly have stayed here ourselves for the night if we had been looking for somewhere but it was too early to stop so we moved on further north.

As we drove along the coast we came across a weird little flower, about the size and colour of a pineapple growing beside the road. The plant (pictured overleaf) was a member of the parasitic broomrape family and is not common and very unlike the broomrapes found in the UK which are generally devoid of any colour and look like washed out orchids.

Impressive broomrape: *Cistanche phelypaeae*

Unfortunately, we soon left this interesting bit of coast and as we travelled north we entered an area which was clearly very popular with British tourists, as the profusion of signs written in English showed. This was the Costa Blanca and it wasn't somewhere which we found immediately appealing. The coastal road was busy and there were villas everywhere and as we entered Torrevieja we were soon surrounded by high rise buildings. Torrevieja, which means "old tower" in Spanish because until around 1800 a guard tower was all that existed here apart from a few fishermen's houses is the main town of the region. In 1803 Charles IV authorised the movement of the salt production offices to Torrevieja from their original position a little further north and at the same time authorized the building of dwellings for the salt workers who were employed at the *salinas* or salt lakes. The population stayed at around eight thousand for about the next one hundred and fifty years then about forty years ago tourist development began and the population grew over tenfold in just a few decades. Jokingly, the region is now sometimes called the "Costa del Yorkshire" because of the number of British living here, many staying all year round and enjoying the mild climate. But not everyone here is British, apart from a smattering of Scandinavians this is also a hugely popular place with the Spanish themselves and this has earned it its other name of "La playa de la Madrid" or Madrid's beach.

We stopped a little north of Torrevieja at Camping Marjal Guardamar, a busy site set on the edge of a godless urban wilderness. We very quickly realised we had made a mistake coming to this place though it was undoubtedly popular. But it was one of those campsites where the pitches were set very close together with no view other than of high rise blocks in the distance. It also had a constant smell of drains which would have been enough to send us scurrying away if it had not been late in the day.

Of course there are things of delight to be found in the worst places and after quite a long walk down a litter strewn path the beach when we got to it was attractive and nearer to the site there was an interesting rubbish-filled drainage canal. This was home to some intriguing birdlife and we could hear a very odd call late into the evening. It might have been a Baillon's Crake, which according to my (unhelpful) book has a call "like an edible frog" which would have been hugely useful if I knew what sound an edible frog made and as it wasn't saying "eat me, eat me" this bird, whatever it was, remains a mystery to this day.

We should have taken the hint from the number of signs written in English and kept driving.

El Campello, Alicante and Benidorm

The following morning we decided another night smelling the drains would be too much so with no outward or even inward signs of reluctance we tore ourselves away from the interesting rubbish and wildlife full ditch and did some serious driving for a few hours, finally stopping just north of Alicante in the district of El Campello, another place where we had visited the previous year though this time we came armed with a better idea where to stay.

We had chosen a commercial aire, "Camper Area Campello Beach" which wasn't at first glance traditionally attractive, being essentially just a large square of white gravel set a few streets back from the beach. But it had very clean toilets, was quiet and above all it didn't smell of drains, though sadly it lacked any interesting ditches for birdlife but we could always catch up with the ornithology somewhere else later.

Compared to some of the places we had seen and stayed at it this wasn't our usual sort of haunt, but we decided to stay here for a while partly because it would to give us the opportunity for some socialising because we found here two couples I knew only by their usernames from the Motorhome Fun Forum. One of the couples, Kerry and Glynn, were full timers in the sense they lived all year round in their motorhome having retired early for a life of travel. They were working part time for a few months at the aire, covering for the receptionist when she went off for her lunch and siesta in return for free board. After several weeks on our own it was nice to have a conversation in English and a good gossip.

A feature of this resort area is an electric tramway running along the coast, linking all the places between Alicante, through El Campello and Benidorm and ending at Denia in the north. It is a modern system and tickets can be bought at major stations or on the train, where there is a ticket machine in one of the carriages.

We boarded at Muchavista, the closest station to us, changing trains just ten minutes later at El Campello station, which was a painless experience as the train we wanted left from the same platform we arrived on. The journey along the coast was interesting, lots of old terracing and fields which were divided up by little low dykes and which were presumably flooded from time to time as a means of irrigation. We could see the remains of a few small aqueducts, of no massive antiquity, which seemed to support this theory. Of course these days nothing is grown in these little fields. Tourists are a better crop to cultivate.

From the train you can also glimpse of some spectacularly vulgar architecture, including a few houses with bright blue roof tiles. This is Spain and to my thinking houses should be white and roofs the colour of the earth. However, I did subsequently discover bright blue roof tiles and other bright colours are not uncommon on church roofs in Spain, so perhaps my reaction was unfair – although they didn't look right on private houses.

A little after an hour after leaving Muchavista we arrived at Benidorm station, itself about one and half kilometres north of the sea front, which is easy to find. Just head downhill from the station and staying beside the main road keep walking in a straight line until you enter the narrow streets of the older part of Benidorm where a small headlands sticks out a short way into the sea.

There are two beaches, a shorter one to the north of the headland, short as in about three kilometres from end to end and a much longer one to the south behind which stand the tallest buildings of Benidorm. The headland is where the original Benidorm fishing village was built around.

Rose Macaulay visited the area after the Spanish Civil War and in an often quoted extract from her book she described the place thus: "crowded very beautifully around its domed and tiled church on a rocky peninsula." These days it's changed a bit. (see next page)

Incidentally, this extract is *all* she had to say about Benidorm as she passed through the area although had she seen the sight we saw (above) from the rocky peninsula she might have had a bit more to say.

The area is of course full of bars and restaurants of all types from Indian to Irish, looking for lunch we found somewhere Spanish serving seafood where I had a cuttlefish. It was very well cooked and tasty which shouldn't have come as a surprise. No doubt you can get poor food in Benidorm as you anywhere else but there are good restaurants here too.

It would be an easy and a cheap shot to be rude about Benidorm, the tandem mobility scooters, the size of some of the folk, but that would be unfair. We just saw a lot of people enjoying themselves, which can't be wholly wrong. Only the uncharitable would think the main value of Benidorm is it keeps the crowds *away* from the more interesting places in Spain.

Benidorm beach scene

Unquestionably, Benidorm is loved by a huge number of people, British, the Spanish themselves and almost every other European nation as well. It's not just the nightlife, in winter this area enjoys one of the best climates anywhere in mainland Europe. Add the weather to the low prices due to intense competition between bars and restaurants and you can easily see why many come here to stay the entire winter, escaping the cold and damp of the UK.

It's just not our sort of place though, far too many people.

Benidorm's shorter beach

Rebujito Nailed

By this stage we had taken a distinct liking to Rebujito and after extended field testing our preferred recipe was as follows:

One part dry sherry which should be Manzanilla but I can't really tell Manzanilla from Fino when they are on their own, add a mixer and unless you have the taste buds of a Jilly Goolden I suspect few others can either.

Two parts lemonade. Sprite or 7 Up is authentic but we have found them a bit sweet. A supermarket *Limón con gas* gives more flavour and a sharper taste.

Ice cubes, the more the better but if you can chill the sherry as we do as well as the mixer this is not so critical which is useful if your refrigerator only has a small ice compartment like ours.

Then the mint leaves. *Hierbabuena* was the recommended type but we couldn't find this originally so bought another and we now have two little mint plants in pots. "Minty" and "Herb" by name. Minty or Menta as it is labelled on the pot was the first we bought and is very clearly spearmint as it tastes like chewing gum. Herb, which was actually labelled Hierbabuena so we were in no doubt we had found the right one, was initially quite difficult to identify but exhaustive tasting in the presence of dry sherry led to the solution, hierbabuena is peppermint. It was a brighter green and with more puckered leaves than the spearmint.

We must admit after much testing we preferred the spearmint to the authentic peppermint, but try both if you can and decide for yourself. I suspect Rebujito is a bit like making a Pimms, there are a few essentials, mint and cucumber for Pimms but after those you can do what you like and I am sure you could be more adventurous with Rebujito, strawberries anyone?

While working on our Rebujito alchemical experiments at Camper Area Campello Beach we received an invitation to visit Kerry and Glynn at their motorhome (which was *much* bigger than ours.) for some paella, that most famous of Spanish dishes.

Kerry was a keen paella chef and she possessed not only a proper wide paella pan but also a special gas burner to use it on. This was nothing particularly complicated, just a circle of tubing with gas jets all around it over which the paella pan was placed but it was a great thing to use outdoors around which the guests could gather, chatting and drinking and watching the cooking, which is what we did.

Spearmint

Peppermint

159

I shamelessly watched how Kerry made the paella in the hope of picking up a few tips. So here is my recollection of how you make a chicken and chorizo paella, I may of course have missed out a few ingredients and give an incorrect description of the method, for which I can only blame the excess of hospitality drank.

Fry onions, add tomato and cook until it starts to go dark red. Probably garlic was added too and then add sliced chorizo and it should look like this (Stage 1).

Paella stage 1

Brown diced chicken in a frying pan, add to paella with stock and sliced beans and bring to the boil at which point wave a bag of rice over everything. Saffron was also added at some stage as well. See photograph Stage 2 (overleaf).

Boil for twenty minutes or one glass of wine. At the end of this time, if you have done everything right you should hear the rice popping and ideally the bottom of the pan should become slightly burnt, this is known as the *socarrat* and is prized by paella aficionados. Turn off heat, add bits of lemon, cover and stand for another twenty minutes or a second glass of wine. When it should look like the photograph captioned Stage 3. Eat and enjoy as it gets dark and the level of wine lowers in the bottles.

Paella stage 2

Paella stage 3

On our final full day at Campello we went for a walk along the long promenade, right to the end where there is the Cap de l'Horta. The distance there was about four kilometres and it took us about an hour to reach it. The rocks at the headland were a soft sandstone with shells embedded in it but this being a Sunday it was quite busy but on the way back we noticed something which to our expectations looked odd. A man was emptying the waste bins all along the promenade, and this was a Sunday. We subsequently learned that bins are emptied quite normally every day in coastal Spain and in some regions the whole practice of using bins is highly regulated. Glass cannot be thrown into recycling bins after a certain time in the evening (too noisy) and general rubbish, which must be bagged of course, can only be put in the communal bins within specific times, which coincide with the period just before they are due to emptied. This is of course extremely sensible in places where daytime temperatures can reach and exceed forty degrees centigrade in the summer. These measures are not just for the benefit of the resident Spaniards, Spain takes its tourist industry very seriously.

Rocky Route

We finally tore ourselves away from Camper Area Campello Beach after a stay of a *full* week. It was a good place to relax if a shade pricey compared to other places but it was very clean and there was a warm welcome which added up to value for money to us. It is certainly a recommended spot to stay and there is more to see there, particularly Alicante itself which is overlooked by a huge sixteenth century castle and where in the Town Hall there is a blue disc on the stairs which is used as a reference point for measuring sea levels all around Spain. Perhaps not the most spectacular of tourist attractions but certainly scoring high in the curiosity stakes.

From Campello we travelled north east along the coast, passing a little inland of Benidorm, which was impossible to miss because of its huge high rise buildings and a short distance later we stopped in Calpe. This beachside town struck us as a genteel mini-Benidorm with lots of English voices around us. We stayed at Mediterráneo Camper which was a commercial aire or camperstop, not as smart as Campello Beach but it offered all we wanted.

The reason for coming to Calpe was a big rock, the *Penyal d'Ifach*, a sort of Spanish rival for the Rock of Gibraltar but without the territorial dispute. It isn't as big as the Rock of Gibraltar either but it certainly dominates the town.

Kerry and Glynn, the paella aficionados, had told us about a path which went from the marina around the seaward side of the rock so on our first afternoon we went for an explore and to try and find it, which we did although disappointingly the path did not go all the way around the rock but it was still a pleasant late afternoon walk.

Bright and early the next day, or at least by our standards it was early being before ten, we set out for the *Penyal d'Ifach*. Although the rock was impossible to miss the route to the bottom of it wasn't particularly well marked or even marked at all until you got very close but if you go to the southern end of the *Playa La Fossa-Levante* beach and then go about two streets inland there are signposts which will guide you towards the Visitors' Centre where there was a little exhibition. The path to the summit of the rock starts from here.

The picture below shows a view of the rock from near the visitors' centre. The path wiggles up through the scrub and trees on the right then crosses from right to left at the bottom of the vertical face of the cliff before entering a tunnel where it emerges on the slope behind the cliff.

The *Penyal d'Ifach*

The sea below the path looked very inviting as we started the walk in sun and with hardly a breath of wind.

Inviting waters

As we got higher we had great views of the surrounding area.

Calpe

The path to the tunnel was fairly well graded and there were handrails where needed but the tunnel was a different matter. It climbs quite steeply (see photograph overleaf) and the rock underfoot had been polished by countless feet so it shone like glass, and it was as slippery as it looks in this picture though fortunately there were ropes strung either side you could hold on to. Without them climbing upwards would have been very difficult.

Unfortunately, when we emerged into the dazzling light beyond the tunnel we were confronted with a sign saying the path was closed beyond this point. Specifically it was closed due to "Works of conditioning".

This didn't come as a surprise to us as there had been warnings earlier and we had asked in the visitors' centre when it would reopen. The answer, while no doubt punctiliously correct, was unhelpful:

"It will reopen when the men have finished the work, señor."

So that was it, path closed for "conditioning" and no further upward ascent possible.

The walk was by no means a failure, the views were spectacular and we had a good sight of what I am fairly sure was a female Dartford Warbler, though not such good a view I had time to get the camera ready. The Curse of the Sperm Whales was clearly still active.

The nasty tunnel

The walk from the camperstop made it a seven and a half kilometres round trip and according to my GPS we reached a maximum altitude of 205m, which was about two thirds of the way to the summit. The walk to the tunnel entrance is graded easy according to the visitors' centre but beyond that it is classed as "difficult" and from what we could see from the end the tunnel they are not wrong. The path was unguarded above a high cliff and worn smooth in places like the interior of the tunnel.

Before leaving Calpe I chatted to the man in reception about the *Penyal d'Ifach* being closed above the tunnel. He said they were constructing a viewing platform or mirador and sorting out the tunnel floor. I suspect falls are not uncommon and broken bones do not tourists attract.

Inland from Benidorm

The bustling activity at Benidorm and to a lesser extent Calpe attract a lot of visitors but just a very short distance away from the coastal strip there is a very different Spain. A sparsely populated region of mountains and gorges which we wanted to visit. So we drove to the little town of Campell in the Vall de Laguar. The name might sound vaguely Scottish but it couldn't be less so.

Campell

The whole area reminded me very strongly of the Alpujarras which we had visited last year. Scattered little villages and hillsides covered in old terracing between deep valleys. On the terraces were a wide variety of trees and bushes bearing olives, lemons, mandarins and cherries. The cherries were ready to eat and we found one with ripe fruit just a few yards from our pitch on the site from which we collected a bowlful. A slice of lemon from another fruit-bearing tree went particularly well with a pot of Earl Grey tea.

Ripe cherries were everywhere

There were also walnuts and (pictured below) almonds.

Almonds

One tree puzzled us, small orange fruits and large leaves, shown in the following picture growing alongside a climbing rose. It is Loquat or Japanese Loquat as it is sometimes known and is a member of the same family as plums, almonds, apricots and cherries. The fruit can be eaten as they are or used in jam as it is high in pectin. Here in Spain it is known as *nisperro*.

What did strike us when we arrived was the amount of birdlife. A golden oriole turned up close to the 'van and when we went for a little wander in the afternoon I saw a woodchat shrike and a bee-eater. The air was full of the calls of birds, which may not sound so attractive at dawn, but compared to the arid regions we had been in recently this place was full of life.

When we left Calpe earlier in the day we drove down a street lined with Jacaranda and it was growing here too. The blue flowers are very distinctive. Originally from South America it has been widely introduced wherever there is no risk of frost. The brown things you can see in the picture below are the remains of last year's seed pods.

Loquat

Jacaranda blossom

The whole of the Vall de Laguar area seems to be full of fonts or roadside springs and just opposite the campsite entrance there was another, together with a traditional village laundry, and very well preserved this one was. The water in the pool was crystal clear.

Village laundry, cold wash cycle only

Plenty of walking routes

There were also very good walking opportunities in the area and the footpaths started quite close to the camp and were generally well signposted. The campsite owner, who had the decidedly un-Spanish name of Ivan, spoke good English and he recommended a circular route which started a little above the campsite then descended through some old terracing which was now covered in trees, eventually it would pass an old leper colony although as events unfurled we never got that far.

Fateful path

We have and use walking poles normally but on this occasion, without a conscious decision on our part, we left them behind. This was something we were to regret. The path ran through the trees growing on the old terracing but every now and again as the general trend of the path was downhill it dropped down to the next lower level of terrace. There were no steps at these points, just a ramp of dry earth covered in places with loose stones like marbles. The path was narrow so we walked in single file; with me leading as I had the map we had been given.

Suddenly, from behind me I heard the sound of Mary's boots sliding on one of these ramps. She fell backwards, putting her hand out to stop her fall. I rushed to her side and realised she had hurt her wrist badly. There is a sort of rule of thumb with injuries, if after a few minutes it doesn't hurt so much then it probably isn't a serious injury. Conversely, if the pain doesn't go away or gets worse the injury is probably not minor. Unfortunately, this seemed to be the case here. I felt completely helpless and could only stand around hoping Mary would suddenly say "it's fine now, let's keep going" but she didn't say it and things were clearly not fine.

Her wrist looked swollen and I feared the worst, bones were broken, so we improvised a sling using a scarf and gently retraced our steps back to the campsite.

Back at the campsite Ivan was extremely helpful and following his advice and directions we drove in the 'van just a few kilometres back down the valley to the little town of Orba where there was a health centre. It was now late morning and fortunately they were still open and hadn't closed for a lengthy afternoon *siesta* yet.

Not being Spanish was not a significant problem for us as there is a European Union wide scheme which offers reciprocal health care to all European Union citizens. The key to getting this treatment is to have a European Health Insurance Card (EHIC) which is free providing you remember to obtain one before leaving your home country, which we had. I handed Mary's card over to the receptionist in the health centre and this was the start of much key tapping on computers. Spain is famous amongst those who live there for being extremely bureaucratic and we were to witness this first hand as the day progressed. We moved slowly from desk to desk and waiting area to waiting area with each stage punctuated by more typing at a keyboard. Eventually we were shown to some seats which looked as though they were outside the doctor's surgery, which they were and after only a short wait we both went in to see the lady doctor. She also typed a lot and quizzed us why we had come here to Orba when there was a health centre in Campell. The campsite had also mentioned this but it was only open one or two days a week and inevitably it was closed today. The lady doctor didn't seem too pleased to hear this and she gradually gave the impression of getting a little crosser with each exchange of information between us. Her English was excellent but she didn't like ours.

"Are you English? Can you not understand what I am saying?" She barked at us at one point for reasons which were completely unclear to us as I thought we had been communicating quite well up until then. Eventually we got to the point we had both long realised was an inevitability. We needed to go to a hospital and get Mary's arm x-rayed and so clutching a wad of paperwork I drove us towards the coast and the accident and emergency facility of the major local hospital on the outskirts of Dénia.

Anyone familiar with hospitals will know excessive parking space is not normally something they are over-endowed with. The answer to the question "Does Dénia hospital have a lot of car parking spaces?" is "Yes" which after a short pause for dramatic effect, is followed by the words "but there are cars parked in them all." We of course were in a six metre long motorhome so even if there had been a vacant space we would have been too long to fit into it. In supermarket car parks the trick is to find two spaces one behind the other so we can fit but if there were two vacant spaces in Dénia hospital car park the chances of them being one behind the other were vanishingly slim to non-existent and we didn't even attempt to look. Parking on the grass seemed the most sensible option and if we got a parking ticket for this offence it would just have been too bad. Having been wheel-clamped once at Winchester hospital a ticket would be almost inconsequential.

Presenting ourselves at the reception in caused yet more keyboard thumping and minute examination of Mary's EHIC card. Failing to find any reason to reject us we were directed to a waiting area, where naturally enough we waited.

The accident and emergency department was as busy a place as they are in the UK and we were glad this was a weekday and not Saturday night during a *fiesta*. Eventually we saw someone who decided Mary needed an X-Ray and entered this requirement into the hospital computer system, after which we told to go and sit down again. After quite a long wait the X-Ray operator appeared and called out several names, including Mary's so in the company of others awaiting irradiation we followed the X-Ray operator along a long corridor and formed up in a line outside the X-Ray room. It was an interesting approach to taking X-Rays, line up all the patients, fire up the machine and zap them one after another as quickly as possible. Was the electricity supplied on a meter and time limited? We never found out but afterwards we returned to the general waiting area again and waited some more.

The doctor showed us the X-Ray on her screen and we could see both the *ulna* and *radius* bones were broken near the wrist. Essentially, nothing was holding Mary's hand on other than skin and a few tendons. We only saw one X-Ray although they had taken two, one from directly above the wrist and the other from the side. The view from above seemed to show all the bones, though broken, were more or less in the right place so the doctor decided it wasn't necessary to do anything to manipulate the bones and a plaster cast around everything would be sufficient. We were both relieved at the time an overnight stay was not necessary but as events were to unfold months in the future Mary's bones were not in the right place and an examination of the X-Ray from the side of the wrist would have confirmed this. At the time we were happy just to leave with Mary's arm well wrapped in plaster, which covered not just her hand but also extended up above the elbow as well. They certainly didn't have any shortage of Plaster of Paris in Spain I thought at the time. The final desk we saw at the hospital wanted to arrange for us to some back in three weeks' time, which we said wouldn't be possible as we would be about to get on the ferry a few days later. The nurse didn't see why this would be a problem. "You can drive to Santander from here in two days." she said and seemed almost offended when we insisted we would leave the area and see our own local hospital as soon as we got back to the UK.

It was early evening by the time we got back to the campsite and I could pour Mary a glass of wine. It had taken most of the day to sort things out after her fall but I could not fault the Spanish medical system. It was bureaucratic but we felt it worked and though at the time we didn't know Mary's injury had not been properly dealt with I am not sure the same might not have happened in the UK. Indeed, much later one of my sons broke his leg badly at work and it was five days and two cancelled operations before there was space in the operating theatre for his leg to be operated on and the fracture secured with a plate. So we will not be critical of Spanish doctors, we may need them again some time.

A caminos rural

Of course, we were now back on our holiday after the medical interruption but with Mary's arm in plaster and in a sling. The cooking side was easy, this was now my job and provided I cut up everything first into bite sized bits Mary could readily feed herself. Showering was a bit more of a challenge but fortunately the showers at the Val de Laguar campsite were quite large and Mary was able to shower herself after I had wrapped up her arm in a plastic bin bag well taped up at the top to make it waterproof. Mary was inconvenienced by the accident but she wasn't going to give up enjoying the holiday and quickly dismissed any suggestion that we could return home early.

As mentioned earlier the area around Campell has lots of good walking, some of it on paths (sharp intake of breath) which we were going to avoid but there was also a network of little roads, *Caminos Rural*, which offered less challenging opportunities for exploration. So a couple of days later we took a circular walk roads along these gentle roads.

Unlike the Alpujarras of southern Spain much of the terracing here was still being actively farmed and around one corner we came across some trees which we didn't recognize. Our first guess was they were Tamarind, as that is what the pods looked like but we discovered later they were Carob. Despite being a tree this is a member of the Pea family. The edible seeds are ground up to make a powder which can be used instead of Cocoa powder and Carob bars are sold as a substitute for chocolate, particularly in health food shops although the most economically significant product from the plant is a gum used in the food industry.

Many of the terraces are still being actively worked although some are abandoned. Cherries and lemons were ready for harvesting everywhere. Some of them with fruit overhanging the road. So tempting to reach out to pluck a ripe cherry...

The terracing is extraordinary, and the back breaking work which must have gone into creating them, probably over generations, humbling.

We also came across the house we had heard about owned by a British couple where they sell jams and chutney from a table on the road outside. We bought a bottle of cherry coulis, which should be nice poured over ice cream and a jar of nisperro jam, which is made from the little orange coloured fruits or Loquats, mentioned earlier.

Later, the sunset made the rocks overlooking the campsite red. We were glad we hadn't rushed home because of something as relatively trivial as a broken wrist.

Very old terracing

Roadside preserves

Back to the Beach – Sagunto

Despite Mary's mishap we had been much taken by the Vall de Laguar. Outside Benidorm's back door there a whole new world to use a hackneyed phrase. It is not surprising that it is being discovered by walkers and a number of companies run trekking holidays in the area. The next valley north from where we were, the Vall de Gallinera is also very worth a visit.

We stayed a few more days at the campsite to ensure there were no problems from Mary's plaster (such as fingers turning blue) and then we continued the northward journey after an abortive attempt to drive westward up to the head of the Vall de Laguar and escape that way. The map showed the road as a dead end but Google maps seemed to suggest there was a way out. There wasn't and we had to do a tight turnaround in a narrow village in order to return back down to Campell and the coast. There *is* a way out of the valley but it goes south, which wasn't the direction we wanted to take. There was no way out north or west without resorting to our feet or using mules.

We took the main road, which runs a little inland of the coast, and drove north. As we approached Valencia we passed through a region, known as the Albufera, of flooded paddy fields, a somewhat incongruous sight in an otherwise arid region. The Albufera, from which the region derives its name, is a freshwater lagoon, the largest lake in Spain and one of the largest around the Mediterranean. The name is a corruption of the Arabic for "small sea" but it has been known since Roman times for good fishing and the surrounding area for productive agriculture. Rice has been grown here since the Fifteenth Century, planted initially by Christianised Arabs. The shallow waters were a breeding ground for disease and the workers lived short lives and eventually depopulation reduced production considerably. Now the waters are free of serious diseases and over one hundred thousand tonnes of rice are produced annually. Rice is the main ingredient of paella and it is from Valencia that paella as we know it now originated in the mid-Nineteenth Century.

We could have stayed on the main road but I wanted to have a quick look at Valencia so I let the satnav take us right through the centre, which I don't recommend you try without something electronic guiding you as signposts were few and far between. After Valencia we skirted around Sagunto, which is overlooked by an impressive fortress before turning off the main road for our destination which we reached by driving through the marshes which lie just behind the coast. Historically, many Spanish towns are set back from the coast on slightly higher and drier ground as the strip between the towns and the coast was a mosquito-ridden swamp. It was only with the rise in tourism that the coast itself began to be developed and the houses, campsites and hotels which we see today built behind the beaches and between the sea and the swamp and sometimes on the swamp.

We stayed nearly a week at Camping Malvarossa de Corinto, a few miles north of Sagunto. It isn't the tidiest of places but it was right behind a quiet beach and our pitch was separated from the beach by only a few bushes through which we had our own private path. It also had reasonably large showers which Mary could cope in one-handed so to speak. It was in the middle of nowhere, with not so much as a bar or restaurant near but it did have its own bar and a little shop where the prices were not too bad and essentials like wine could be sourced.

One day as we walked along the gravel beach we came across hundreds of little fish stranded along the tideline.

Stranded little fishes

It was an unexpected discovery and my assumption was they had been chased into the shallows by a shoal of larger fish and in their haste to escape were left stranded.

As my earlier description of making paella was somewhat influenced by the effects of alcohol on my memory here is another go

179

at describing how to make this dish. It doesn't matter it is a vegetarian one, the method is more or less the same whatever you use. The only difference being if you were using meat it may need to be pre-cooked a bit to ensure it isn't served under done. Had I been around when the fish jumped out of the sea I might have been able to gather some and use them but lacking any little fishes here is a description of how I made for our last night by the beach a vegetarian paella.

Slice and dice some onion and add to pan with some olive oil. Sweat until it softens a bit.

Sweated!

Then add chopped garlic and when that has softened a bit add chopped pepper, courgette and diced aubergine. Gently fry this in the oil after adding spices, I used a ready mixed paella spice but smoked paprika would do on its own. Then add tomato purée, chopped tomatoes, vegetable stock and I also added the saffron but this isn't essential if using a sachet of paella mix as it will already be included but we had some saffron so I added extra. Bring to the boil. A splash of white wine didn't do any harm either though I didn't the entire carton in - the chef needed a little refreshment.

Gently fry

I then left it to simmer for exactly the time it took to have a shower, drink a cold beer and open up a bottle of what I thought was red wine only to discover it was a bottle of Muscatel, a bit like sweet sherry. Nice but not an ideal match with paella and certainly not when warm. Fortunately, we still had a "brick" of Conde Noble in the 'fridge so all was not lost. Finally add the rice and cover with foil and simmer for twenty minutes then leave to rest for another twenty minutes, add extra water if required, but aim to get the rice to absorb all free liquid. And it was very tasty. The description above might give the impression it takes a lot of effort to make paella but this really is not the case. The method is essentially one of throwing everything in the pan and cooking until ready. The only skill, if it can be called that, is getting the timing roughly right and deciding when the different ingredients are thrown in the pan. Of course, to make a *really* good paella, with the correct *socarrat* does require skill but even my feeble efforts produced something tasty and unlike a typical risotto it didn't all taste the same like baby food. The bit I probably didn't get right was the cooking of the onions and tomato which are supposed to be cooked gently with garlic to produce a tasty and soft *sofrito*.

Serve and eat

Paella was originally a food of farmers and labourers and was perhaps a forerunner of today's one pot meals. There are a few competing theories for the origin of the name. The most likely is it comes from the name for the dish, derived from *patella*, which is Latin for a pan and is also the medical name for the kneecap, no doubt because of its dish-like appearance. Another theory is it originates from the Arabic for "leftover". The final theory suggests it means "para ella" meaning "for her" and it was a dish cooked by a man for his lover. This is probably a bit fanciful but it is true men do often cook the dish in Spain especially outdoors.

While we were at the site a curious conjunction of astronomical events occurred. For a couple of evenings the moon rose in the east at almost exactly the same time as the sun set in the west. The result was the red sunset cast a red light over the rising moon. The photograph below is a composite of two exposures. I tried taking a single shot but to capture the sky and clouds the moon had to be over-exposed and if the moon was correctly exposed the sky was too dark. The answer was to take two shots and combine them, which is what I did and it gives a better impression of what we could actually see with the naked eye than I could achieve with a single photograph.

Red moon at night, shepherd's confusion

We did a bit of sunbathing on the beach most days, which always presented something new to look at. A ten minute walk south on the beach took you to an official naturist beach or *playa nudista* as the signs showed. It was more or less deserted during the week but on our last Sunday there it was positively heaving with bare bodies, some of whom must have come some distance as the local population wasn't that large. Not that the naturist sunbathing was confined to the designated area, folk stripped off anywhere along this stretch of coast from what I could see and there was a constant *leakage* of people from the *playa nudista*. An intriguing couple we saw every day started off in the nudist section and then walked all the way up the beach past us, following the waterline, hand in hand until they reached some buildings several hundred meters further north of the campsite. Here they turned and walked back to the *nudista* section. They repeated this two or three times then got dressed and drove away. For some reason their actions reminded me of a people I heard about when we visited South Africa once. The *strandlopers* were an indigenous people (now extinct) who lived by literally beach combing, walking along the beach each day foraging for food. Given the climate of South Africa I suspect they were similarly unclad like our Spanish couple.

Finally – Gassed

For the previous couple of weeks we had been slowly running down the on-board gas tank until by the time we left Sagunto it was well into the red on the dashboard gauge. Although it hadn't actually run out yet I thought we would give it one more chance at filling. So we found another Repsol garage with autogas and tried again. And…it worked. We took on board a full tank of gas and I can only assume the pressure in the tank, although not completely empty, was lower than it had been during earlier attempts to refill and the pressure difference between the inside and outside was sufficient to blow open the sticking valve. So in the end we didn't need the loaned gas bottle but its presence had given us great peace of mind. Thank you Richard, who did eventually get his bottle and regulator back when he visited the UK many months later.

The title of this little section might not mean anything to non-motorhomers but the idea of being "gassed" in a motorhome has grabbed the attention of the popular press from time to time. The typical story has a couple who awake one morning in their motorhome to find they have been robbed. They had not been woken during the night and even their dog apparently slept through the raid. Lacking any obvious answer as to how this could have happened they usually decide they must have been "gassed" during the night. Unfortunately, local police officers called to the scene of the "crime" sometimes agree with the victims' solution to the robbery, it's a lot easier than arguing in a foreign language which reinforces in the minds of the victims that they must actually have been gassed during the night and they were robbed while unconscious.

It makes a good story in the newspapers especially, as often seems to be the case, wallets containing a lot of cash and the odd expensive watch are also taken at the same time.

That someone could be gassed in a motorhome is of course quite possible, but are they gassed? The Royal College of Anaesthetists has issued a statement which succinctly and convincingly says they don't believe a word of it. Their main argument against "gassing" ever having taken place is no one has died in one of these incidents. You could say this is very fortunate, but it is more than that. When the Russians pumped an anaesthetic gas into the Moscow Dubrovka Theatre in 2002 where 850 hostages were being held nearly 20% of the hostages were killed. Some probably died from an overdose of the unknown gas used but others would have choked because if you fall unconscious lying on your back then there is a good chance you will swallow your tongue and die as a result. Other arguments put forward by the Royal College of Anaesthetists are the sheer cost of an anaesthetic gas sufficient to fill a motorhome, the lack of any residual smell in the morning and the lack of any blood tests carried out which might have shown the presence of an anaesthetic. Despite the strong scientific argument that it just does not happen there remain those who simply cannot think of any explanation other than gassing to explain their loss so they are totally convinced it must have happened the way they think it did.

The rational solutions are that a proportion of these reported cases may be insurance frauds but the majority will have a much simpler explanation. Either the motorhome owners forgot to lock the vehicle and the thief quietly opened a door, reached in and removed everything which was conveniently to hand or the items reported missing were lost somewhere else. This latter is not so fanciful and you can easily imagine someone going to a bar or restaurant and after paying their bill falling into the clutches of a pickpocket as they leave the premises. The next day they find their wallet missing, so it must have been stolen during the night while they slept. No, it was stolen before they returned to their motorhome.

Albarracín and Goodbye to Beaches

Although in a sense, Cabo de Gata had been the "turning around" point in the trip, in that it was as far south as we went and everything subsequently had been taking us back to where we had started from, it hadn't felt like we were going home when we were enjoying a paella near Alicante or sitting on a beach at Sagunto. But inevitably, this being a trip with a finite end point, the date of the ferry, we had to admit our real return had started when we left Sagunto and the Mediterranean and drove away from the coast, heading north west on a route which would eventually take us to Santander and the ferry to Plymouth. This was the final leg of the journey.

Our route was initially directly towards Zaragoza on the main road but this was no hurried retreat, there was still time for some diversions to places of interest. Inland Spain has a huge amount to offer and it is a great pity so many folk simply regard it as a space to drive through as quickly as possible, a bit like Belgium, or fly over in their quest to stay by the sea so before we got to Zaragoza we turned west onto more minor roads at Teruel. We were heading towards the remarkable town of Albarracín, which is a popular place for tourists but we were not going to let that put us off because I knew it was somewhere special. Zaragoza and Albarracín are at the southern end of Aragon, a region which has an enormous variety of scenery, stretching from the snowy Pyrenees in the north to the arid mountains in which Albarracín is found. Aragon, which stretches almost half the length of Spain is a relatively under-visited region compared to the coastal strips but it has much to offer and Albarracín is one of its jewels.

We had enjoyed excellent weather since leaving the north west of Spain and our brief stopover in Portugal but the rain began to look as if it was going to finally catch up with us. There were several squally gusts after we arrived at Albarracín and the sky looked ominous in the evening. With less than ten days left we decided over a glass of wine the best plan was to continue moving north in little jumps. I would have loved to return to the Pyrenees but the forecast for the coming weekend was not good. Rain we can live with, no such thing as bad weather, only unsuitable clothes and all that but as we realised on our first journey impressive views are not much good if you can't see them. So we decided we would take a lowland route away from the high mountains on our return to the north coast.

But first we had Albarracín to explore and after visiting the Tourist Information Office (which was open, we usually find them closed) who gave us a map from which we chose a path to try which ran beside the river and looped up and around the far side of the town. The path started off level after we had crossed a decidedly wobbly bridge supported on cables but then there was a steep, rocky bit, which given our recent mishap on a sloping path and Mary's plaster encrusted arm ensured we turned back at that point.

This photograph might help to show where we were. Old Albarracín is in the background, with the Arabic fort further back still on a rocky hill. The path we attempted is just below the centre of the photograph, meandering through low mounds. The houses in the foreground are the more modern new Albarracín.

Albarracín

However, on the short bit of the walk we did complete we came across an interesting waterwheel which was lifting water up into a small aqueduct. It was a clever little engine using the main force of the stream to turn the wheel around the rim of which were affixed little vessels. As the wheel rotated the vessels were filled with water as they dipped into the stream then near the top of their rotation they poured their contents out into a trough running alongside the wheel. Very clever and similar designs can be found in places like Syria and Afghanistan.

So with the path forbidden to us we walked up and into the narrow and winding streets of the town where one of the first things that struck me was they had some impressive doors. Old Spanish towns major in old doors as do Italian ones, it may be a Mediterranean thing about keeping daughters well secured or probably just a way of keeping the unwelcome visitor out. Some of the door fittings were superb.

A skilled blacksmith made this

Impressive doors

Who is it?

The town is protected by a deep ravine on one side and a high wall on the other. The church bell tower had brightly coloured tiles on the roof, something which I had been rude about near Benidorm.

A well protected location, Albarracín

There were of course a few tour groups but not many and the place was delightfully peaceful. As it came up to one o'clock the skies darkened so we sought shelter in a restaurant, unfortunately it must have been the chef's day off as it was a pretty mediocre meal, but no matter. We sheltered from the rain and thunder which went on all through lunch and the meal came with a full bottle of wine to keep up spirits. None of your wimpy little jugs here. The following day we took a waymarked path up a ravine. The path started just behind a building with a large fibreglass dinosaur on the roof near the campsite. It was some sort of dinosaur museum but the business was firmly closed and looked as if it had gone bust, though not before someone had clearly invested a lot of money in the venture, which was sad, if only for the bank which had lent the money.

The path we followed led along the bottom of a gorge or *barranco* for the first couple of kilometres before becoming a path through woodland. The sides of the gorge were made of red sandstone which has been heavily shaped and coloured by water and the weather.

Weather worn rocks

Purple salsify *Tragopogon porrifolius*

The valley had lots of evidence of previous cultivation with walls, ruined buildings and terracing throughout the valley floor. Some of it was still being used and one tiny bothy had been restored and was probably a holiday or weekend place for someone. We also came across a few beehives but they looked abandoned with no signs of occupants.

There were lots of flowers blooming including some Marsh Orchids but one flower in particular was very striking, being nearly three feet tall. It was *Tragopogon porrifolius* or Purple Salsify (previous page) which has has an edible root like a thin carrot and is sometimes grown by gardeners as an alternative to carrots.

Going Up

The following morning we moved all of about 30 kilometres from Albarracín to a campsite near the town of Bronchales called Las Corralizas which is the highest campsite in Spain at 1750m. This fact, when I read it came as a bit of a surprise to me as I had previously thought the honour of the highest campsite belonged to the site at Trevélez in the Alpujarras, south of Granada, but it seems Trevélez is only a mere 1550m. Trevélez is reached after climbing up narrow winding roads amongst high mountains, the road to Bronchales, while a bit narrow in places gave no hint of the altitude. The explanation is the centre of Spain is a sort of rough plateau, the *meseta centrale* with an altitude of six or seven hundred metres so it doesn't take much climbing above that to reach relatively dizzy altitudes.

Our drive from Albarracín, especially the first part where the road followed the River Guadalaviar (not to be confused with the similar sounding Guadalquivir) in a narrow gorge was particularly interesting and I really should have stopped to take some pictures, especially as, unusually for Spain, there were plenty of places to pull over.

High camping - Las Corralizas

We arrived at Las Corralizas in fine weather but shortly afterwards, in the way we had become so used to on last year's trip the clouds came, thunder and lightning were let lose by the Gods and then hail, which was particularly noisy hitting the 'van roof lights. The rain water formed rivers running across the ground and at any moment we expected to see our Crocs, which we had left outside, floating away into the distance. The storm went on for some time and thunder was still rumbling around several hours later.

Fortunately, the weather improved around five o'clock and there were even brief intervals of sun which gave me a chance to do a little gentle exploring around the rocks jutting up out of the ground beside the campsite. The vegetation was very varied, with broom, mountain willow, juniper and a prostrate cupressus of some sort.

The bird life was quite varied too, I saw a pair of Rock Thrushes and there was a little yellow bird which might have been a Citril Finch but it wouldn't stay still long enough for me to get a good look at it.

In one corner of the rocks I came across a curious little shrine which was fairly recent in origin I think but it was clearly well known and a number of people had left home made crucifixes all around it.

Mysterious shrine

Going Down

We left Las Corralizas in sunshine after a somewhat chilly night which had me turning on the heater for the first time since we had left Galicia. The first half hour of the drive was a bit chilly too, as it was virtually all downhill and the engine took ages to warm up.

We passed through Daroca, filling up with fuel and where we hoped to do some shopping but the GPS didn't know of any supermarkets within twenty five kilometres of the town. However, the kindly lady at the garage pointed me towards a supermarket very close by. Even with her directions we almost missed it as it was very well hidden without any signage on the road. It was called "Simply Basic" and indeed it was, being a sort of cash and carry. Not a lot of choice but it was cheap.

Daroca is worth an explore, it has the remains of old walls made of mud but it was lunch time and getting hot so we moved on and parked at the visitors' centre at the Laguna de Gallocanta for some lunch. This is Spain's largest natural lake (not counting the Albufera lagoon by Valencia) but it is peculiar in that it can almost dry up at times and indeed did so in the summer of 1969. Technically, it is an endorheic lake, meaning it has no outflow and any water draining in can only leave by evaporation. As a result the water is salty and the shores white with salt.

The lake is famous for being a stopping off point for migrating cranes and apparently eighty percent of the cranes of Western Europe pause here during their migration from Africa. Unfortunately, this being June any cranes in the area which might have been visible would have been on building sites although there quite a few birds on the water, which looked very shallow. The birds were a very long way off and hard to identify through the heat haze but were probably black winged stilts.

After lunch by the lake we drove to Nuévalos, south west of Zaragoza, along a very bumpy A2506 road. Our map showed another lake, the Laguna de Zaida nearby but we could see nothing of it. Subsequently, looking on Google Maps the mystery of the vanishing lake was explained. The map does indeed show another lake a little to the west of the Laguna de Gallocanta, but switch to satellite view and the lake is replaced by some ploughed fields although the outline of the former lake is still just visible.

Laguna de Gallocanta - crane central

At Abanto, a little town off the A2506 there was a building by the side of the road made of mud bricks.

Mud house

Where we were at this point is shown on the map below. Aiming for Santander but with still time for the odd diversion off the direct route.

A Walk in the Park and Chocolate

We stopped for the night at the campsite at Nuévalos, a town on the banks of a very large reservoir. The site was about five kilometres from the Monasterio de Piedra which we intended to visit the next day. The monastery is in theory walkable from the site but it is uphill all the way along a busy road and after smelling the drains in the toilet block while having our morning showers we decided we would not stay a second night at Nuévalos and would move on after we had visited the monastery. Not the first time the smell of drains had persuaded us to accelerate our plans. Not that the site was a bad one, it was just a bit smelly in the plumbing department.

So next morning we drove to the monastery, along with half of Spain it seemed as the car park when we reached it was almost full. It was of course a Saturday so if you plan to visit, which I recommend you do, my advice would be to avoid weekends as the vast majority of the visitors were Spanish folk out for the weekend. Of course, "avoiding weekends" is sound advice almost anywhere in Spain.

The entrance fee was a steep fifteen Euros and to be blunt the monastery itself is nothing special. Construction started in 1195 and it was built largely from stones filched from an Arabic castle which had previously stood on the same site. The monastery had a somewhat turbulent history and was finally abandoned in 1835. It was privately owned for a while and part of the monastery is now a hotel. Of what remains, some bits are attractive and others are a bit run down if not downright derelict. The hotel part, from what we could see of it didn't look anything special either.

The monastery has one special claim to fame, the popularisation of chocolate. Although Columbus was the first to discover the cacao bean he seemed to know nothing of what to do with it. It took a monk from the Monasterio de Piedra to spread the word and Father Jeronimo (or Jerome) de Aguilar was the instigator of the chocolate revolution in Europe. Aguilar was part of the force responsible for the conquest of Mexico but he lived amongst the Maya as a slave for several years, having been captured after a shipwreck. It was during this period that he learned, not only the Mayan language but also how to make chocolate. When the Conquistador Hernan Cortez landed near where Aguilar and his companions had been shipwrecked he heard tales of bearded men and thinking they might be Europeans he investigated and subsequently bought Aguilar's freedom from the local chief.

Although he subsequently never left Central America Aguilar sent in 1535 several sacks of cacao beans to the Abbot of the monastery together with a recipe for the making of chocolate. It was a huge success and the monastery became the first place in Europe to make chocolate. The kitchen today is still an interesting place to visit, circular with a domed and blackened roof with a hole in the centre it now houses a sort of chocolate museum where there was an old device for roasting cacao pods, which was fascinating though it clearly didn't date from the time of Cortez.

Early chocolate bean roaster

The cacao went in the spherical vessel which could be rotated over a fire and swung to one side away from the fire for filling or emptying or just to control the temperature.

Underwhelmed as you might be by the monastery and wondering if you have wasted your entrance fee the real reason for coming here is the park, which consists of a walk below, along, through and above a series of cascades and lakes which are mainly natural but have been tweaked by Man.

As it was so busy (another weekend) we more or less shuffled round in a line of people all intent on photographing each other and their children.

The cascades are largely natural

The walk starts in pretty parkland. Then it becomes a bit more challenging, disappearing into tunnels with lots of steps. Through windows in the tunnels you can see out into the park.

The path then goes behind a waterfall, which you take at a sprint to avoid getting wet. Beyond this is another tunnel, thankfully dry inside though it was wet under foot. When you emerge from the tunnel you soon cross the bridge which was visible in the shot on the next page. Looking back you can now see the full waterfall.

Looking down from the waterfall

Airy drop to the right – and the waterfall

"We came through there"

It may be hard to see but about three quarters of the way up the waterfall there is a wooden rail. This is where the shot looking down onto the bridge was taken. The wooden rail can also be seen in the picture showing a man with a rucksack. The path then drops down inside the cliff further and goes behind the waterfall near the bottom, where there is a dark gap to the left.

After this excitement the path takes a much gentler route past the fish ponds which fed the monks. In the UK monks dined on carp but their Spanish brothers seemed to have fared better with trout, large trout it seems as some of the fish in the ponds must have been approaching five pounds in weight. They sell fish food at the entrance and if you come this way I suggest you buy some and help the fish grow even bigger.

One of the lakes

There is then a long spring fed lake with crystal clear water.

It was a good day out and worth fifteen Euros a head and providing you are reasonably fit (lots of steps) and not too troubled by vertigo or claustrophobia it is very enjoyable. And if you are troubled by any of those just make certain you have someone nearby to hold your good arm at the tricky bits.

Leaving the monastery we drove north west through Monteagudo de Las Vicarias to Almazan (south of Soria) through the most striking scenery. It was like the Wild West with "mesas" sticking up, flat topped and steep sided. Unfortunately it was raining most of the way which both detracted from the view but also accentuated the "other worldliness" of the region.

We then spent a couple of relaxing days at a campsite a little west of Sofia beside the large Embalse de la Cuarda del Pozoa, which is popular for sailing and other water sports. The site is in a pine forest and it took a bit of searching to find a level pitch. Note the chained gas bottle in the picture below and the two pots of mint by the back wheel.

Camping in the pines

The Rio Lobos and Glacial Lakes

Leaving this site after three nights we drove a short distance to San Leonardo de Yargüe, a town with an interesting name and a dark link with history.

During the Spanish Civil War the town of Badajoz, close to the Portuguese border, west of Mérida in the south west of Spain, was besieged by some of Franco's troops under the command of Lieutenant Colonel Juan Yargüe, who with the aid of German Junkers Ju52 bombers broke into the town and confined the defenders in the bull ring. Executions then started and the total number killed is estimated to have been between two and four thousand which included wounded men in hospital. Yargüe earned the sobriquet "the butcher of Badajoz" for this action.

Yargüe was a contemporary of Franco; they both received their commissions at the same time at the Infantry Academy in Toledo. Yargüe and his troops led a revolt in Ceuta in North Africa at the very start of the war before crossing at the Straits of Gibraltar to join the other Nationalist forces at Seville, before going on to the massacre at Badajoz. An action which hardly damaged his career, he ended up as a Lieutenant General and Minister for the Air Force and the town where he was born was renamed in his honour.

These days the town despite its off-putting name is quite an interesting place to visit with an aire by the main road to the east and a little Carrefour, where we did our shopping. It is also where we set off to visit the Cañon del Rio Lobos which is a short distance to the south, but before this, we stopped at the conveniently placed *fuente* to refill our water bottles, and very good water it was, we were still drinking and enjoying it several days later.

In the canyon we parked by the bridge of the seven *ojos* which means "eyes" which is shown on the next page, notice the stepping stones nearer the camera. You might also notice in the picture the complete absence of the Rio Lobos herself. The mystery was explained on a conveniently placed sign which is reproduced below.

The seven-eyed bridge

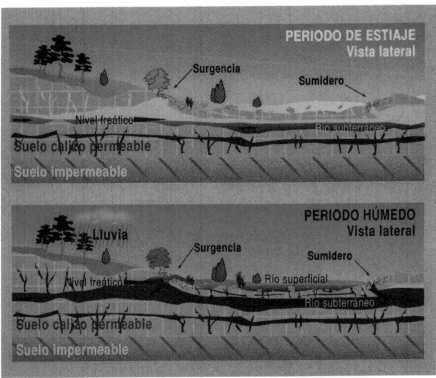

"If you can see the river it has been raining"

The river is largely subterranean at this point and only overflows onto the surface during periods of high rainfall.

The cliffs above the river showed a lot of evidence of water flowing through them. In the picture below you can see, apart from the cave formed by the river that at this point the river itself was visible on the surface, though there was no discernible current. There was also quite a lot of debris which had been left by a recent flood. The river then vanished a little way further downstream, sinking back down into the river bed.

The now-you-see-me-now-you-don't Rio Lobos

There were lots of footpaths in the area and the one we followed was level and easy walking. There were flowers in bloom everywhere and in the air were several griffon vultures. By the car park a raven was croaking away.

The flowers were attractive too. The Rock Rose on the following page is possibly *Cistus laurifolius* but the other species we saw defeated me, other than knowing there was some sort of Euphorbia and a Geranium. The lack of a suitable flower book didn't help as it isn't until you get back to the UK and look them up that you realise you can't really do it from the photograph because you don't know if the stem was say hairless or square in section and you didn't photograph the leaves properly at all.

This is all a very interesting area and worth a longer stay. The origin of the name Lobos might mean wolves but it might also be a corruption of the Arabic word for a plank, meaning a place which is long, narrow and flat. The valley floor is certainly flat and the Arabs did get this far north but perhaps the origin of the name is now lost. It is certainly somewhere to come back to, if only to see the remote little Hermitage of San Bartolome tucked away in the *Cañon*, which we missed, but a ferry beckoned and we moved north from here, going back to San Leonardo of the nameless one where we took the very minor road north towards Vilviestre de Pinar. The lower stretch of this road has been recently resurfaced and it was a superb. As an aside there are possibilities for wild camping just north of the village in several picnic areas.

Rock rose

Continuing north on the narrow road we passed through Quintanar de la Sierra, a sizeable town and headed for the Lagunas de Neila which are a group of glacial lakes near the summit of a mountain. You get tarns like these in the Lake District, usually called something like Blea Tarn and are formed when the retreating glacier melts.

The road up to the lagunas was shown as unsurfaced in my atlas but it isn't, although it has quite a few potholes and is very steep, first gear all the way for us with only a few sections where I could get it into second. This being a Monday there was virtually no other traffic and we didn't meet anyone coming down while we were going up. Like the roads we had been driving on since leaving San Leonardo they are barely wider than single track. You could pull over and stop to let a car squeeze past but anything larger and someone would have to reverse, probably quite a long way.

Just before the end of the road there was a mirador or viewing platform which looked out over the nearby and not so nearby hills.

The view point is above a high cliff protected by a low wooden fence. Below the fence were two bouquets of recently cut red roses. It was difficult not to speculate on what might have happened here. The drop behind the fence was sheer and went a very long way down.

At the end of the road was a small car park, but no visible lakes, for these you have to walk and from the path there were glimpses of another smaller lake below.

Little tarn

It was about a kilometre along the path to the first of the larger lakes, the aptly named Laguna Larga. At this point the link with the Lake District, which the picture below shows very well, became quite real as we were quickly enveloped in low cloud so we turned around and headed back, which meant we missed Laguna Negra, the black lake and the most well-known of the lakes but it was by now mid-afternoon and we hadn't had lunch yet. Fortunately, the cloud soon lifted and we could drive down safely, albeit on a wet road from the rain which had also arrived with the clouds.

Laguna Larga

From the lagunas we drove north again, rapidly descending from the 1840m at the top of the lagunas' road. It was first gear for long periods to save the brakes with the engine rattling away at nearly 3,000 rpm and deafening us.

The road we chose followed the Rio Najerilla down a narrow, steep sided canyon for a long way. I should have stopped to take pictures but it was raining (again) and I had grown soft after several weeks in the sun. However, it was a very interesting route with lots of signs warning of falling rocks and indeed little and some seriously large rocks were there to be seen by the side of the road.

A Pause for Wine

Joining the modern world a little west of Logroño we scooted a short distance along the motorway before arriving at Haro, which is famous for its wine festival, to be held here just two weeks after our arrival, great timing on our part although I suspect the campsite would be full during the festival. This wine festival is no highbrow *degustation*, it starts at the crack of dawn with a Mass and then all hell breaks loose with folk throwing and squirting wine over each other. In Spanish it is known as the *La Batalla del Vino* – or Wine Battle. Then around midday the battle ends and everyone goes to the bull ring to chase young bulls and heifers, which is followed by dancing, eating and drinking into the night. Sounds like our sort of day, if we were forty years younger.

We stayed at the popular Camping de Haro, beside the Rio Ebro. This is quite a swish site with neatly trimmed hedges between the plots and was stuffed with British caravans and motorhomes. We met up with a couple who were on the last site we were on and there was also a Dutch couple here who we last saw at Albarracín, it's a small world.

The reason for going to Rioja, which was the region we were in, is of course the wine, which they take very seriously here. There are about a score of *bodegas* in the city and many of these are conveniently within walking to and staggering back distance from the campsite.

We are new to wine tasting so we were a bit put off initially by the closed front doors. "Are they open?" We asked ourselves and the answer is they were and you just had to push open the doors.

This was *Muga* who seemed to have the biggest bodega in Haro and with the cheapest wine for sale at €12 a bottle we had a quick look around, took a photograph and left. The phrase I used above, "staggering back" I was beginning to think might apply more accurately to our reaction to the prices rather than over consumption of the product. But they did have a nice little steam engine on display outside.

We then found *bodega Cuna* which conveniently has its own car park opposite should you wish to stock up your car or motorhome before departure. Going inside we found the days of free wine tasting have passed so we elected for the €15 option, which gave us five wines to try. The other option was €25 for just four wines from their up-market range.

Bodega Muga - the outside

Bodega Muga - the expensive inside

As our wine tastes are more bodega Lidl we think we chose the better option for us. Fortunately, it isn't €15 per person and you can share, which is what we did, this being mid-morning and drinking on an empty stomach is usually unwise, as we found out afterwards when we walked out into the fresh air.

The wines were not all poured at once of course, the guy in charge, who spoke excellent English described each wine and how and where it was made.

Wine tasting in progress

The wine on the right is a white Rioja, fairly easy to spot as they had conveniently written the colour on the label. White Riojas are not often seen in the UK but they should be as this one was really nice and not outlandishly expensive at €7 a bottle, although it would be twice that in the UK I suspect. The most expensive red was €23 a bottle and aged two years in the barrel, but was too dry and tannic for me.

But your tastes may differ. It was an enjoyable morning and another place to come back to. We ended the day with a €3 bottle of a rosé Rioja from the camp shop which was also very good. I didn't know they made a rosé in Rioja either but we liked this one (dry and fruity) and so we bought a case before we left the next morning, which was our last day in Spain.

Back to the Ferry

Our route from Haro to Santander was the N232 which despite being an N road was extremely twisty and narrow in places, riddled with potholes in others and delightfully free of traffic. There are also minor roads running through the mountains which parallel it but we didn't have the time for this option.

Shortly after leaving Haro the N232 vanishes for a moment and we had to use the N1 for a short distance, and what a very different type of road. This seems to be the main route for freight arriving from the rest of Europe heading for Madrid or Portugal. The only requirement it seems for driving on the N1 is to have a forty foot articulated truck as there was very little traffic of any other sort to be seen. This was not a road I would have liked to drive on very far and fortunately after a few kilometres we could turn off it and back onto the re-born N232. The final hills where it becomes the N623 take you over the Puerto del Escudo at 1100m and then over a fairly short distance you descend down to more or less sea level. I just selected a low gear and let the engine do most of the braking. We had crossed over the Cordillera Cantábrica again as we had returning on our first journey, the long range of mountains which separates the moist, green north of Spain from the rest of the country.

We headed initially not for Santander but for Torrelavega where there is a collection of supermarkets all conveniently close to each other on the eastern side of the ring road. The Carrefour sign is very noticeable from a distance and the others are close by. Beware there is a height restriction on the main entrance to the Carrefour car park although I think there is another way in around the back. We did most of our shopping at Lidl and then parked outside Carrefour and walked in for the few extra bits Lidl didn't think we needed.

It was now late afternoon and although the original plan was to try and have a look at the new aire which has opened on the docks at the end of the runway we gave this a miss and went straight to the port. Parking beside what was to become a long line of at least a hundred plus motorcycles. I talked to one biker who had done a more or less complete circuit of Spain and Portugal, mainly wild camping and completed it in ten days. He had had a great time he said.

Waiting to board

Then a big, familiar looking boat arrived.

"This will take us home"

Eventually we were called forward for passport checks then lined up again for a further wait. As seems often the case we were more or less the last to get on but we are used to that and we were soon making ourselves comfortable in the Piano Bar before having a very pleasant meal in the restaurant.

And that's more or less it. There were no whales or dolphins to be seen unfortunately, partly as we woke in the morning surrounded by fog, although this did eventually clear by mid-morning. All in all, it was a very calm crossing and after nearly eight weeks chilling out we took the enforced need to sit still in our stride. Our full route is shown below.

Appendix 1

What is Motorhoming?

A motorhome, campervan, motorcaravan or in the language of North America an RV, can at its simplest be a van with a mattress thrown in the back with a bucket for a toilet (optional) and a portable gas stove for cooking (also optional). At the other end of the scale it could be a vehicle the size of a bus costing hundreds and thousands of whatever currency you like to choose. All have some features in common, they are self-propelled in the sense of having an engine and don't need to be towed like a caravan, they have somewhere to sleep and in all but the smallest vehicles a toilet/shower and a kitchen. Of course numerous options can be added, heating, satellite television and awnings to give shade for example, but the basic motorhome remains just a mobile house you drive to new places and in which you can put your head down for a night's sleep.

Our Motorhome

Our motorhome is a Murvi Morocco, made just a few miles from where we live in South Devon. It is six metres (twenty feet) long, sleeps two and has an excellent large kitchen and a toilet compartment big enough to have a comfortable shower in as well. Storage space is a little limited but this just encourages us to reduce clutter and take only what is essential. I have, though, fitted a large storage box on the rear which carries our deck chairs, the insulated cover for the windscreen (great when it is very hot) and numerous smaller items such as the ground sheet and the hose for filling with fresh water.

After trialling a few options we now sleep under a duvet, just as we do at home. It is easy to wash the cover and we get a comfortable night's' rest.

Which Motorhome?

The smallest motorhomes are little bigger than standard cars and they have the great advantage of being easy to drive and parked anywhere a car can. The downside is their kitchen and toilet facilities, if present at all, are generally a bit basic although this isn't always a problem and small campers remain very popular. The classic surfer's VW is a good example of this type. For us, being a bit soft I guess, we chose more or less the smallest motorhome you could buy which had a full sized kitchen and toilet/shower. You can get ones a little shorter with these facilities but this is generally at the expense of even less storage space.

There is no such thing as the perfect motorhome. One widely voiced maxim is "they are all a compromise" which refers to the trade-off between the various features of a motorhome. Within a given size of vehicle there is a design decision which needs to be made on how to divide up the available space. A large sleeping area with a permanently fixed bed means less space for other features. To get around this and make a larger "living room" the bed can be made to fold away. This immediately gives more space but the bed needs to be made up every night and with a couple they are inevitably required to go to bed at the same time. Of course if you buy a large motorhome it is possible to have both a fixed bed and a large space for lounging and entertaining but apart from being more expensive the compromise is such a vehicle can be a challenge to drive on narrow roads and park in confined spaces such as those you might find in a mountain village. An alternative bed configuration is the drop down bed where a fully made up bed winds up into the roof of the vehicle and is lowered when required. Motorhomes are made in all different sizes and internal layouts simply because not everyone's requirements are the same. Our model wouldn't suit a lot of people and of course many of the motorhomes I see on the road wouldn't suit us either. We are all different and that is a very special thing.

As this isn't a book about choosing a motorhome I will leave the subject at this point. I can only suggest if you do plan on buying a motorhome try not to follow the route all too many have been down which is to buy one and discover on your very first trip there is something about it which not only do you dislike but decide it is so bad a feature you can't live with it either and a different vehicle is needed. This can be an expensive mistake but one quite a lot of people make. If you have been camping or caravanning before you probably have a reasonable idea about living with your loved ones in a confined space. If you haven't then renting a motorhome first would be wise. Renting is expensive but it is a lot cheaper than the loss you will probably make changing your motorhome for another shortly after you bought it.

Appendix 2 - Where We Stayed

Note: Aires are generally listed on the Dutch website www.campercontact.com and are referred to by their site code number. So CC10222 is site code 10222 on the campercontact website. There are several websites which lists places to stay but CamperContact has a very easy to use app for both Android and iOS which will work off-line. It lists reviews of most sites, machine translating them where appropriate.

Where We Stayed – 2014

15 September, Camping Portuondo, Mundaka. www.campingportuondo.com

16 - 18 September, Camping Zuriza, Anso Valley, Western Pyrenees. www.campingzuriza.es

18 - 22 September, Camping Malvarrosa de Corinto, Sagunto, near Valencia. www.malvacorinto.com

22 - 24 September, Camping Bonsol, Alicante. www.campingbonsol.es

24 - 26 September, Camping Bellavista, Águilas. www.campingbellavista.com

26 - 28 September, Camping Don Cactus, Motril, Malaga. www.doncactus.com

28 September - 1 October. Camping Valdevaqueros, Valdevaqueros, near Tarifa. www.campingvaldevaqueros.com

1 - 5 October. Camping Playa Las Dunas, Puerto de Santa Maria, near Cadiz. www.lasdunascamping.com

5 - 7 October. Camping Playa Taray, Isla Cristina, near Spanish/Portuguese border. www.campingtaray.com

7 - 9 October. Figueira Caravan Park, Figueira, Western Algarve, Portugal. www.figueiracaravanpark.com

9 - 10 October. Aire at Puerto Gelves Marina, Seville. CC10222. www.puertogelves.com

10 - 13 October. Camping El Sur, Ronda. www.campingelsur.com

13 - 15 October. Camping Balcon de Pitres, Pitres. www.balcondepitres.com

15 - 16 October. Camping Despeñaperros, Santa Elena. www.campingdespenaperros.com

16 - 17 October. Aire in Valladolid. CC22431

17 - 18 October. Aire at Navia. CC19284

18 - 22 October. Camping Perlora, Candás, near Gijon. www.campingperlora.com

Where We Stayed 2015

20 - 21 April. Area del Lago del Acebo, Cabarceno Wildlife Park. CC6016

21 - 22 April. Aparcamiento Puerto Chico, San Esteban. CC25916

22 - 24 April. Camping Poblado Gaivota, Playa de Barreiros, near Ribadeo. www.campingpobladogaivota.com

24 - 25 April. Parking Pabellon de Deportes, Lugo. CC18677

25 - 26 April. San Pedro de Visma, Car park at port. CC5848

26 - 27 April. Cabo Fisterre, Rough parking area at end of track. CC24664

27 - 28 April. Praia de Mañóns, parking area. CC15051

28 - 30 April. Area de Besadoiro, Sanxenxo. CC18988

30 April - 1 May. Area de O Mundil, Outomuro. CC15343

1 - 2 May. The Citadel

Bragança. CC5362

2 - 4 May. Camping Don Quijote
Cabrerizos, Salamanca. CC26715
www.campingdonquijote.com

4 - 5 May. Area de Talavera
Talavera de la Reina. CC19894

5 - 7 May. Camping El Greco
Toledo. CC40086

7 - 8 May. Camping Los Batanes
Lagunas de Ruidera. www.losbatanes.com

8 - 9 May. Cazorla Forest
Small car park in the middle of the Cazorla Forest. Coords not
recorded.

9 - 12 May. Camping Los Escullos
Los Escullos, Cabo de Gata. www.losescullossanjose.com

12 - 19 May. Camping Bellavista
Águilas. www.campingbellavista.com

19 - 20 May. Camping Marjal Guardamar
Guardamar. www.campingmarjal.com

20 - 25 May. Camper Area El Campello Beach
El Campello. www.camperareacampellobeach.com

25 - 27 May. Mediterráneo Camper, Calpe.
www.mediterraneocamper.com

27 May - 1 June. Camping Val de Laguar, Campell.
www.campinglaguar.com

1 - 8 June. Camping Malvarrosa de Corinto, Sagunto.
www.malvarorinto.com

8 - 11 June. Camping Ciudad de Albarracín, Albarracín.
www.campingalbarracin.com

11 - 12 June. Camping Las Corralizas, Bronchales.
wwwlascorralizas.com

12 - 13 June. Camping Lago Resort, Nuévalos.
www.lagoresort.com

13 - 16 June. Camping Urbión, Abejar.
www.campingurbion.com

16 - 17 June. Camping de Haro, Haro.
www.campingdeharo.com

Appendix 3

Suggested Reading and Sources of Information

Guide Books

We have become fans of the DK or Dorling Kindersley, Eyewitness Travel books. They are up to date, very well printed and have lots of clear illustrations. One feature we have found invaluable in their country guides is at the start of each section they list the highlights in each region together with a good map showing where these highlights are to be found. We used these frequently to plot our route. We also used this feature perversely, deliberately choosing an area on the map where there were no obvious highlights. This is a sure-fire way to avoid the crowds and we were rarely disappointed with what we found.

DK Eyewitness Travel: Spain - The main book we used.

DK Eyewitness Travel: Back Roads Spain - A useful description of scenic drives through Spain to give you more ideas on possible places to visit.

DK Eyewitness Travel: Northern Spain - With a bit more detail than their general book on Spain. There are also some specific DK books on the main cities and the surrounding region which are worth looking at. For example, if you wanted to visit Barcelona they have a book about Barcelona - and the surrounding region of Catalonia.

The Rough Guides are well produced and worth carrying but though once a fan of the Lonely Planet series I rarely use them now. In my opinion they are often poorly printed, with near illegible maps and are aimed more at the back packer looking for nightlife and cheap accommodation. Yet, all these books are still worth looking at if you have the time before you leave as each carries at least some information not included in the others.

I didn't use any campsite guide books other than the Caravan Club book on touring in Spain and Portugal. This certainly doesn't cover all sites but it did list the odd one I couldn't find anywhere else, so making this book worth having.

The main source of campsite locations for us were the ACSI books (www.campingcard.com) which were invaluable.

For books on aires there is only one I am aware of, published by Vicarious Books and is called "All the Aires Spain and Portugal". Though a lot of information is available on-line these days nothing beats a hard copy book when your electronic device has a flat battery. The aires listed in this book and their other country guides, are also all inspected by the publishers so you should have an idea what to expect before you arrive.

Maps

The Michelin Road Atlas for Spain and Portugal, though not as well printed as their laminated equivalent for France is perfect for day to day navigation. For general route planning a big map of the whole country you can unfold is essential and the Michelin 1:1,000,000 map of Spain and Portugal takes up very little room but has enough detail to be useful for navigation as well.

For larger scale maps those produced by Marco Polo are good though they do not cover the whole of the country.

Language

Not my strong point but I've found the various BBC Active audio books best but there is a very wide choice available from other companies.

Books About Spain

Chris Stewart's "Driving Over Lemons" series are strongly recommended. These give a wonderful insight into life in the Alpujarras. Available as both paperbacks and eBooks.

Gerald Brenan's "South from Granada" is a very readable and interesting account of a remote part of Spain just after the First World War. Available as an eBook.

Laurie Lee's "As I walked Out One Midsummer Morning" describes his adventures after he arrived in Spain penniless and on foot up to the outset of the Spanish Civil War. It is one of his best books but if you have any aspirations to be an author beware of reading it. His prose is sublime, like liquid poetry and my efforts are primitive scratchings in crayon by comparison. Lee's follow up book "A Moment of War" written much later has become somewhat controversial as there is a suspicion some of it is fiction, but it is still worth reading. If it is fiction then Lee writes good fiction.

Jan Morris wrote "Spain" shortly after the death of Franco so there is little about recent Spanish history but it is exceptionally well written and the potted history of the country at the beginning is concise and evocative.

On-Line Resources

Apart from the obvious search engine - used frequently both before and during the trips there is one outstanding motorhome forum in the UK: www.motorhomefun.co.uk which I have used extensively when planning trips. There is a great deal of knowledge in its large membership but they are also very helpful when something goes wrong. It was through this forum we borrowed a gas bottle when we had technical issues in southern Spain. There is no doubt had we had other problems we would have had no shortage of helpful advice. I strongly recommend before venturing anywhere in a motorhome you join this forum.

The Dutch website www.campercontact.com was also used frequently for finding places to stay, more details can be found in Appendix 2.

www.john-laidler.co.uk

Printed in Great Britain
by Amazon